A noted spiritual writer,
lection of meditations on just about every theme of Christian concern. In His Presence *moves with simple ease and honesty from theme to theme and reflects the author's compassion and understanding for humanity and humanity's problems. Below is a sampling of the critical acclaim for book and author:*

"72 brief meditations . . . on topics pertinent to modern Christian living . . . The reader may find himself saying: 'How true!' or 'I must remember how he put that.' Each one will find his favorite meditation." *America*

"[Evely] does say much of the same thing from one book to the next; yet the message somehow is always fresh, compelling, sobering. . . . Like the gospel message he preaches so ardently, he seems never to go out of style." *The Sign*

"Meaning and limitless application characterize Evely throughout all of his writing, and the present volume is no exception. His constant themes–life, Christianity, brotherhood, and holiness–must be woven together in one's life." *St. Anthony Messenger*

"As always, [Evely] writes incisively about the Christian life in today's world, his insight applying equally well to the ancient Gospel and to our present circumstances."
Msgr. John S. Kennedy

". . . a book written to remind us of God's continual Presence among us, and we can never get too many reminders of that." *The Catholic Messenger*

Louis Evely here offers a col-

In His Presence

LOUIS EVELY

Translated by J. F. Stevenson

IMAGE BOOKS

A Division of Doubleday & Company, Inc.
Garden City, New York

Image Books edition by special arrangement with Seabury Press
Image Books edition published September 1974

Original edition: *Dieu et le prochain*,
published privately by the author

Nihil obstat: JOHN M. T. BARTON, S.T.D., L.S.S., Censor
Imprimatur: ✠ PATRICK CASEY, Vicar General.
Westminster: 13 August 1969.

ISBN: 0-385-06002-5

Printed in the United States of America

Contents

In His Presence

The Creator and Evil

The only God I know and love is Jesus Christ.

For me the Creator is an alien being, one to be dreaded, filling me with anxiety. "This God," said Christ, "no man has ever known him." Only the Son has entered deeply enough, boldly enough, into relationship with him, into his confidence, to dare to call him Father.

For the great modern religious problem is perhaps that of the creation. Contemporary atheism is a passionate phenomenon; it springs from a furious revolt against the misery of mankind and of the world.

For a long time we Christians have tried to make do with the answer that the world was good and that the responsibility for all the evils we suffered belonged to man's sin alone.

But that is over and done with; a moment's thought and, above all, geology, palaeontology, etc., have proved beyond any possibility of doubt that evil existed here below long before sin and before the creation of man.

The world God created was cruel, catastrophic, monstrous, ruthless, rocked by earthquakes (Agadir was no sin of man's, it was the Creator's!), shot through with atomic radiation (all we have done is to intensify it), swarming with deadly germs; it is based on a savage struggle for survival, it crushes the weak, it squanders countless lives and sufferings, a world glowing with heat or ribbed with ice, the graveyard of million upon million of species.

No, there is nothing very "reassuring" about God. I imagine him as an artist of genius who gets an idea, then makes and tears up thousands of sketches: a terrifying cosmic power, beyond all measurement, a stumbling-block. In his presence I can feel admiration or fear but certainly no goodwill!

It is perfectly true, I know, God could not have created a perfect world. He would have been creating nothing at all since he would have made nothing distinguishable from himself.

But the question remains: why did he choose a world with such a degree of imperfection?

For long ages, man in his weakness pledged to his Creator, to Nature, a devotion full of fear, an unconditional awe, a total submission. You kissed the hand that struck you as the hand that gave you alms. (A parish priest from the north once said to me: "My parish is tough. It is suffering from a hundred years of good works!") In the old days everybody hit you: the lord hit his serf, the boss his workers, the father his children, the parish priest his flock. In Canada there is not a single adult who does not remember a redoubtable kick somewhere or other, delivered by a parish priest, a brother or a nun. They have all been marked, as it were, basically, by clericalism!

So if God in his turn handed round a few blows, administered a bit of correction here and there, it never occurred to anyone to be surprised at it; in fact one always found good excuses for him. One bowed one's head and respectfully kissed his terrible hand!

But modern man has discovered his own dignity and renews across 2000 years the pride of Christ, asking his executioner: "Why do you strike me?"

The first thing that characterizes the modern attitude to the world is a movement of revolt and compassion before its "absurdity," the swarming forces of evil, the cruelty of the way it is organized. And the second is that man has grown aware of his own strength, he has got the feel of his own power; he no longer thinks of just sitting there and admiring the world; he feels capable of transforming it, of doing better.

Pascal, gazing up into the star-filled sky, could still say: "The everlasting silence of that infinite space appals me." He was afraid, he was awestruck, he was thinking of God.

The man of today, as he gazes up into the star-filled sky, is on the look-out for his satellites, is planning interplanetary voyages, is working out each stage of his route. He is thinking of himself.

But above all, to me as a Christian it seems that the principal divine attribute is not made manifest in creation: mercy! Christ said: "Be perfect as your heavenly Father is perfect. And be merciful as he is merciful," thus showing clearly that the summit of perfection is mercy.

But nature is *merciless*.

I would never have been the priest of the Creator. I am cowardly enough to fear power, perhaps I am cowardly enough to admire it, but nonetheless not abject enough to love it, to prostitute myself to it. The Creator could have imposed on me his laws, his restrictions and, of course, his punishments. Obviously I would have had to submit, but once I had paid him what I owed, I would have been quit of any further obligation—let him not ask over and above from me the slightest goodwill!

It is only in Jesus Christ that the countenance of God has been made manifest to me.

It is only through the Redeemer that I receive light enough to endure the darkness that for me surrounds the Creator.

In the presence of God made vulnerable, weak, suffering and serving, in the presence of that child or that crucified man to whom I can do all the hurt I want and who will never pay it back, I too am disarmed. I have no more words to say. I accept the belief that God is a Father and that he suffers as I do, more than I do, from his creation.

No, God does not will evil. No, God does not do evil: it

"does not please him to recall his servants . . ." and he does not send us trials like a calculating and cold-blooded pedagogue.

And it is even scandalous to say that God *permits* evil, like a Pilate washing his hands of the blood of slaughtered innocence. If God permits the suffering of one single being when he could prevent it, I am an atheist.

The truth is that God fights with all his strength against evil, God suffers to the depths of his being at our evil and he inspires all those who weep at the evil of the world, who hunger and thirst after justice, who struggle like him to free the world of evil.

God is only love; everything happens in the world as if God were weak. The devil is strong: he is rich; powerful, hard, invulnerable. God fights against the devil without armour, without weapons, bare-handed, with raised visor and uncovered face; he fights only with his love. But do you know any greater strength than this of daring to be so weak? Power can kill but only love calls forth life.

Parents or catechists who waken a child to adoration by making him the slave (for three months the slave of the catechism!) of the God of nature, of his power and his majesty, are making him a Christian for the reasons for which he will at the age of eighteen become an atheist. If it was God who created roses and sunsets, it is also God who is responsible for germs, volcanoes and tidal waves.

One must believe only in Jesus Christ!

In Christ I believe there is a victory of love over evil and suffering, and that if God is not justified by the beginning of his work, he will one day be blessed for its consummation. The true paradise has to be built and we shall one day be astounded at all we have been empowered to do by his confidence and inspiration.

I give thanks to Jesus Christ for having revealed to me the human countenance of God and that Power of love which is stronger than all evil.

"Only a suffering God can help us."

Man in his destitution spontaneously imagines a God at the opposite extreme to himself, a God who is rich because man is poor, powerful because man is weak, autonomous and self-sufficient because man is dependent, a God invulnerable because we suffer. But then man is given over once and for all to his most abject ambitions, his basest longings. He would like to become like *his* God.

But Christ frees us by revealing to each one of us that to become God we do not have to become rich, strong, powerful, solitary, unfeeling; it is enough for us to love and to serve. You can become God as from this very moment: begin to love, to suffer, to serve like him!

Saving one's Soul

Far be it from me to present the religion of the Saviour as one of "every man for himself!" We are Christians not in order to be saved but in order to become saviours. The gift of God increases our responsibilities, and salvation demands greater generosity within the Church than outside it.

And yet the words of the Gospel remain true: "What does it profit a man to gain the whole world if he suffers the loss of his own soul?"

It is so easy to lose one's soul! It gets lost in prayer that grows dry, empty, narrow, becomes introspection, illusion, egoism ("I say 'my' prayers!"), routine. A great deal of praying is a turning in on oneself far more than an opening of oneself to God. Saying prayers is often an excellent way of not praying and one's soul is lost in activity, in restlessness, vanity, self-interest. (It is strange how one can be simultaneously empty and weighed down! It is when one is filled that one's heart is so light!) How quickly we get to the point of doing simply, when the whim takes us or necessity compels, the things which we began to do because it was our duty! How we seek out affection from those to whom we ought to give it! How clever we are at exacting payment for our devotion, initially so pure, by complaints, moodiness, a tyrannical caprice, self-pity, or the art of getting our devotion noticed.

"A vulgar person," said Schiller, "is interested in what he does." (One can go on down the degrees of vulgarity with "in what he feels, in what he possesses, in what he appears.") But a noble person has eyes only for what he is, who he is. "Who is the person who does what I am doing?"—that is the important question. The most precious moments, the truly blessed hours of existence, are those in which you let your soul return, in which you begin to exist again, in which you fill your action with the best of yourself. It is then that what you are doing becomes an integral part of you and enriches you.

One is so rarely the person that one loves to be! We move around habitually as if bereaved of ourselves, as alienated from what is truest in our own selves as we are from others. It is a gift of grace or of chance, that state in which our faculties are released, in which is restored to us the power to dispose freely of that which is most intimately our own. Man becomes himself only by chance. He grasps a truth only by inspiration. He discovers himself only by surprise. Who will open up to us the landscape of our inner self? How shall we be melted down, made one, fruitful and happy?

I believe that the whole art of living, the whole reward of experience and culture, is the discovery of what I call one's "resting places," that is to say, the means of becoming again the person that one loves to be.

We have all noticed how, after a long talk with a particular person, we come back to life, we are confident, we are renewed; once again everything in our life seems clear, the world is good. Every province of our nature breathes again. We are reconciled with ourselves and with others. We know once again why we live and that it is good to be alive.

But the same thing can happen to us also after a long walk, or when we are standing looking at a landscape, or seated on a tractor ploughing an endless field of brown earth. At heights above 10,000 feet, a man is changed, his heart grows lighter, he becomes simpler. And what the previous generation found in churches and chapels many seek today in mountaineers' huts, on skis or at sea.

My soul returns invincible when the music of Bach is playing or when St John is speaking. I cannot go on hating or stay turned in upon myself if I re-read that poem or look at that picture. A particular book is there, in my library, and I know that if I re-read it it will convince me once again that I must stop being spiteful or pessimistic, it will bring me into its world, into my own true world, but the outcome is so certain that I often find myself hesitating to open it for fear of the wrench which I dread. And a particular prayer, in the same way as the greatest masterpieces, communicates to me the state of soul of the man who composed it.

Happy is the man who has provided himself with food for his journey, who bears with him through life the secret of reconciliation to himself and of becoming again and again unceasingly the person that he loves to be.

A child is the plaything of circumstances; in order to find himself he waits for circumstances to change. When he has "lost himself," he has lost everything, that is to say when he has lost the way to those persons from whom he draws his life. His suffering is without remedy because he has no means of acting on it and foresees no end to it.

But the adult exercises his power on events. It is not always possible for him to change his conduct, to alter his state of mind, to guarantee his perseverance by a pure decree of his will. But he does well to place himself in circumstances and under influences such as to render him vigorous, generous, cheerful and faithful. He can become himself again by those means which he knows well from repeated trial.

That is what maturity is, the art of swiftly returning to that depth at which it is good to be alive and to which youth gets down only intermittently.

A true religion is precisely one which teaches us to live in this state of grace, which leads us towards those secret things that slake the soul's thirst, which gives to its movements ease and grace, which open up to it the dimension of depth.

We should make a constant effort to live surrounded by those means revealed to us by art, nature, religion, culture and friendship, which create or guard our living soul.

There is no other way of "saving one's soul!"

And it is simultaneously the greatness and the weakness of the human soul that it can come back to life, that it can be itself, only in virtue of the loftiest inspirations, in the company of the genius, the artist and the saint.

Predestination

Catholics no longer dare speak of predestination ever since the Protestants took the word over. But St Paul says that we have been chosen before the creation of the world and predestined by God to be his adoptive sons. And the sole ground of our confidence is that free, gratuitous and loving choice. For what reason would he love us if he did not love us for nothing? And why should he cease loving us if he began to do so without cause?

It seems to me that there are two stages in the spiritual life. The first is one of pride, in which one says: "It's not worth getting up, I'll fall again just the same; there's no point in aiming so high, I'll soon be back in the mud; it's a waste of time cleansing myself, it won't take me long to get defiled again."

And the second is after one has had experience of the faithfulness of God's love, and one says: "There is no point in just going on lying on the ground, I am bound to get up sooner or later; it's no good trying to shut myself up in my sin, God won't leave me alone. I won't be able to go on forgetting him indefinitely, I won't resist him for ever. However long I go on turning a deaf ear, the moment is bound to come when I let him persuade me once again to return to him."

In that case, I might as well get up straightaway; I might as well not be obstinate. I know myself; I know that I lack perseverance in evil even more than in good. Because, if God has once chosen me, he still chooses me unceasingly. His choice is always active, his will for me is stronger than my sin.

Those who trespass against us

Often, when we say the "Our Father," we come to an embarrassed halt; nobody has trespassed against us, we have no grudge against anybody. Isn't it worrying to ask God to forgive us who have so offended him, as we ourselves forgive, in the void, in the abstract, those who have offended us?

We can, however, find something better to do. There

does exist one person who has disappointed and injured us, a person with whom we are everlastingly dissatisfied and whom we pursue with a bitterness we would never dare to direct at any other: that person is ourself.

We are so fed up with ourself. We are nauseated by our mediocrity, disgusted with our lack of consistency, wearied by our own monotony. The relationship in which we live with this closest of all neighbours whom God has entrusted to us to guide and offer to himself, is one of unbelievable coldness, even of hatred.

We would never dare to judge any other creature of God with the contemptuous neglect with which we overwhelm ourselves. And yet one is bound to love oneself and it is said that we should love our neighbour as ourself.

We must therefore ask God to teach us to pardon ourself, to soothe the rancour of our pride and the disappointments of our ambition. Let us ask him that the loving-kindness, the tenderness, the indulgence, the unbelievable confidence with which he pardons us, should spread to us, should penetrate us in such a flood as to carry us upon its tide.

In the last analysis, we only know that we ourselves are pardoned when we begin to pardon in our turn. The only proof that we have received forgiveness is that we have learned to forgive. We cannot know the love of God for us without our mind and heart changing towards ourself and without granting him against ourself the benefit of the doubt when he loves us.

Getting oneself killed

A place in which time passes slowly, one single place in the midst of our restless life, those jet-propelled weeks that are gone before we even notice, a place where we have time to live, where time can be tasted, broken down into moments, and each moment full of sap; a unit of achievement, a relaxation into a life truly to be lived: that is prayer.

I don't mean either ecstasy or rapture. A monotonous calm, a sort of just-bearable suffering. A process, as it were, of continual crushing, of regular grinding down, of persistent repression, of that awkward, clumsy, ungainly, vacuous personage that we are for ourself.

Every minute digs away, erodes, assaults, represses, casts out that restless, hard and unhappy being that our way of life has made of us. To offer oneself, to expose oneself to God the whole time, as a man puts his head out of the trench under fire, to see whether the moment has come to be killed. . . .

To pray is to run the risk, to take the chance of getting killed. "Come on, Lord, when will you kill him, this dreary stupid being? When shall I be rid of it for ever? Look, I am lifting my head, I am looking at you, calling you, provoking you, isn't it yet the moment to die?"

The time passes slowly and peacefully, endlessly renewing the opportunity and the intention. And in the long run under that pressure, that incessant wearing down, and thanks to that salutary pain, there is a strange communication of life. We thought of dying and we begin to live. God gives life while killing. Precisely that part of ourselves that we thought good for nothing save death is the point at which, beyond all understanding, we begin to love and to give thanks. The dry bones come back to life. Within the perished flesh, grace freely circulates. We shall never have ended, we shall never have had enough of getting ourselves killed like this.

Creative Love

The family is a place of paradox; in it one is loved very much more than one deserves. The moral law that rules the affections and prescribes that each one should be loved to the extent that he is worthy of it is deliberately violated. Within a family people love each other without hesitation far beyond what each is worth. And to be loved, to be accepted in this way, creates in the bosom of the family incomparably greater happiness and kindness than anywhere else.

Those who truly love us do not love us by reason of the qualities we possess at the moment they encounter us but in virtue of the kindness, sensitivity and prescience of their own heart which feels certain, patient, strong enough to waken one day in us a love like theirs. To love a person is to address to him the most powerful and imperious form of appeal, it is to stir up in the depths of him a silent and hidden person forced to emerge in response to our voice, so new that even its owner did not know it but so true that he cannot fail to recognize it, even though seeing it for the first time.

Praying

To pray means to put oneself at God's disposal. To let him for one moment do in us that which he from all eternity wills to do and which we never grant him the time to do. We are like those sulky and obstinate children whom their parents would dearly love to forgive, to bring to a confession of and a great regret for the fault committed. But the children can't believe it, won't trust, cling to their isolation, avoid every occasion of being alone with their mother, pretend not to understand her promptings, manage always to have a third person with them when in her company. Because otherwise, they know perfectly well, if they let things take their course, if they were to listen to her for a while, remain alone with her, well! that would be dreadful; they would at once want to ask her forgiveness, they would start to weep and to be sorry all at once and they would know, lo and behold, that she had already forgiven them. It would be because she had already forgiven them, because she longed to tell them so, that they were brought to ask forgiveness themselves.

God is like that, God is as good as that. God desires to give us very much more than we are willing to receive. He waits, he is patient, he watches for the moment when, at long last, we will consent to allow him to begin in us his work, when we will put ourselves in his terrible and fatherly hands.

When you go into a church, when you kneel down to say a prayer, you should shout for joy and laugh with happiness to start with. God is at his work; look, God is working in you, he has already begun to break down that resistance that you endlessly offer him. He has already won his first victory over you, this unbelievable gesture of having turned to prayer; and now, if you remain, if you wait long enough, you are going to know, you are going to learn how God has already heard your prayer.

The Infinite Egoist

"God created the world for his glory," the catechism teaches us.

So people say to themselves: God is like us, he refers everything to himself, he is busy with his own interests and creates for his own advantage. As he is manifestly stronger than us, there's no alternative to submitting and accepting the sacrifice of our egoism for the benefit of his. Actually we are also told that these two egoisms coincide because he created for our happiness also. Everything is indeed for the best in the best of all possible worlds. What an elevating ideal it is to model ourselves on his example in promoting our own interests, the more so in that everybody gains by it.

But the glory of God is neither the extension of his power nor the manifestation of his wisdom; it is the revelation of his love. The glory of God is to be Love, the greatest love of all, the one which gives life and which gives its own life.

The glory of God lies not in receiving but in giving. God creates the world out of charity so that other beings should live with his life, rejoice with his happiness, imitate his generosity and so come to know the very taste of God's own joy which is in giving. God is gift to the point of granting us to be gift in our turn. God is Father to the point of granting us fatherhood, that is to say, to be God for other persons. It is in this that we give glory to him; by loving each other as he has taught us to by dint of loving us himself. The glory of God is in having sons. If he had no sons, he would not be Father, but his sons resemble him only if they too become fathers, become God in their turn.

Heirs of Heaven

Children learn in the catechism that sanctifying grace makes us children of God and heirs of heaven.

Christians are very privileged people. They not only have in general an inheritance to hope for on this earth but also another one, promised them in heaven. It is a sort of super-capitalism. We simply rake in the profits. We turn heaven into a bank.

Heirs? Of what? God possesses only one thing: he is Love. He knows how to love and to give. Our inheritance from him will be the capacity to love and give in our turn. It is a fine sort of inheritance that makes you give everything you hitherto possessed! An inheritance to be accepted with reservations! The only sign that we are heirs of heaven, the only proof that we have inherited from God, is our being able to give whatever it is that we have managed to accumulate up to now. There'll be no question of hoarding here! The only sign that we have passed from death to life, says St John, is this, that we love our brethren.

The Everlasting Alliance

Don't you find the redemption very disappointing? It has changed nothing in the conditions of our life that are the result of sin. It is a concealed redemption, a redemption for later on. Everything takes place under the veil of faith as if the redemption were unreal, as if matters were deliberately arranged to make it unverifiable, as if it had never happened, as if only sin had left a lasting mark on the face of the earth. Why has the redemption not restored to us what Adam lost for us?

And yet salvation is far more wonderful than the earthly paradise. The order which it establishes is irrevocable. One sin was enough for Adam to lose for ever all that God had conferred on him. For us, on the contrary, grace is inexhaustible.

It is true that our redemption takes place in humility; it is not wrought by exemption from sin (as we would like it to be), but in the forgiveness of sins. Only, this forgiveness is unceasingly offered. We are bound to God by an alliance from which he will never withdraw. Our redemption establishes an order of grace characterized by an unbelievable generosity. Since God loves and forgives us without our deserving it, our faults will never deter him from loving and forgiving us. It is true that we can suspend for a time certain effects in us of his love and forgiveness. But we cannot abolish them and once we yield again to the grace which urges us to turn to them, we shall find God all the more joyful at our return and the more compassionate for our greater wretchedness.

Why should we envy Adam? He had the earthly paradise, we have Jesus Christ. He had received a gift from God, we have for ever the promise of his inexhaustible forgiveness. He lived . . . it is no longer we who live, it is Christ who lives in us. He was a "friend of God"—we are sons in the Son of God.

Doing without God

The fundamental sin of man lies in his fear and hatred of God, his revulsion from God. The worst sin is not the recognition that one cannot observe his commandments. The worst sin is to say to God: "I couldn't care less about you; I just want to pay no attention to you and to have you leave me alone. It suits me fine to be where you are not. I'll get by as best I can, but without you." The worst sin that many people commit against God is perhaps the desire to commit no more sins so as not to be forced any longer to go back to him for forgiveness.

Even people who say their prayers use them in general with a view to becoming one day capable of doing without him: "Give me that, and I'll leave you in peace."

We go to confession in order to get rid of the duty of confessing, so as to be all square, to be quit and free. Quit of whom? Free what way? We excommunicate ourselves in the very act by which we propose to be restored to grace. God's forgiveness, instead of revealing and overwhelming us with his loving-kindness, restores us to that good opinion of ourselves that we should like to have.

But those who have truly been forgiven have never thereafter left the confessional.

They spent all their life with their confessor. They felt no desire to run away, hugging their forgiveness. They found God so good that never again could they depart from him, for he to whom nothing is forgiven does not love. He to whom a little is forgiven, loves a little. But for the man to whom much is forgiven, there inevitably comes the time when he has learnt to love much.

Withdrawal

We all of us have a diabolical taste for nothingness. We live under the endless pressure of a temptation not to be, to destroy ourselves, to draw back from a certain communion (with God and with others) outside of which we know quite well that there is no true life.

Man was drawn forth from nothingness and he will always keep a terrible longing to return to it. That, it seems to me, is what pride is. Those who define it as an inordinate esteem of oneself know nothing of its passion and its frenzy, its content of desperation, hatred and ferocity. They are confusing it with an innocent vanity. What pride desires is to be self-sufficient, to cut off all communication and exchange, to stifle in its own solitude, to feed on itself without appetite, to drink itself without thirst. "I smell bad but it's *my* smell; I taste flat and stale but it's *my* taste; I drown in sadness, but it's *my* sadness."

We come from God and we go to God. It is by no means pride, as people think, but rather humility that is needed for us to consent to go to God, to belong to God, to become God. To open oneself to another, to depend on another, to be happy only by reason of another—this is terrible for us. It is so much easier to be unhappy all by oneself. Nothing and nobody are needed for that. The damned soul is the one who has got to the point of total withdrawal, of absolute self-excommunication.

Faith, hope and love are inherent in the soul, but the soul unceasingly fights against them. Man goes on believing that unbelief, hatred, despair and hardness of heart give him a deeper access to his essential self.

But what is the point of turning in on oneself, of possessing oneself, if one becomes thereby incapable of giving oneself?

To possess oneself, to be rich with oneself, means before all else to be possessed by oneself, as the rich man is possessed by his own riches.

The only possession worth having is the capacity to give oneself. Truly to possess oneself means to be in one's own gift, free of self, capable of giving oneself, capable of trust and love.

Our personal subsistence is the residue of a certain incapacity for giving. Each person of the Blessed Trinity is subsistent relationship. But we subsist as individuals, exclusive and incapable of being wholly given.

Our autonomy is not so much a power as something that weighs us down.

Adam sinned not because he was weak but because he was a man. It was hard even for Christ to conform his will to that of his Father.

God alone is able, with the fullness of his energy, to set his heart upon Another.

God and Evil

Perhaps the greatest problem today is this: Is God worthy of the suffering of men? An impassible God, smug, safe in his heaven, wallowing in his happiness? What an impoverished state, what a wretched idea of God for men subject to suffering, proud of having suffered and desiring no solidarity or communion save with those who suffer like themselves.

But it is precisely we Christians who despise a self-centred happiness, an individual salvation on the lines of "every man for himself," a solitary and self-sufficient God

(*Non in unius singularitate personae*: not in the isolation, the egocentricity of a single person, we rejoice to say in the preface of the Holy Trinity.).

We believe that God is gift, communication of self, love; we believe that in God the worst forms of human distress find something that gives them a brotherly welcome, something which is worthy of them, we believe that our surest path of communion with God lies through suffering and that it is only through the equivalent of the most exacting human renunciation that one wins through to the incomprehensible bliss of God.

Suffering and happiness are infinitely less contradictory than impassibility and love. He who imagines God to be unconditionally happy commits the worst sort of infidelity against him; God loves, God is the most reckless being in the universe; he has set all his happiness in his love, he has made all his happiness depend on another, on whom he has set his heart. That is why he could only reveal himself to us in sorrow. The joy of God emerges from the greatest suffering. He gives his life for those whom he loves. There is no greater love, there is no greater suffering, there is no greater happiness than that of giving one's life for those one loves. Such is the only happiness of God.

God is vulnerable

God is Love. Love is vulnerable. To love a person is inevitably to depend on him, it means giving him power over you. God has freely loved us, God has given us power over him. God willed to need us.

The Passion is the revelation of our terrible power over God. He gave himself up to us, we had him in our power, we did with him whatever we liked. On plates in Normandy you can read this cruel and cynical proverb: "The strongest is he who loves the least." It is always the one who loves less that orders the other around, keeps a cool head, stays in control of the situation.

God, in relation to us, will always be the weaker because he loves. God can be denied or forgotten; he cannot deny or forget us. We can carry on living without God. God cannot be without men.

We can cease to be sons, he cannot cease to be Father. "Man in his revolt against God is like a bird in the storm, dashing itself against the cliff, but God in his compassion became flesh so that the force of the blow should be taken by him and not by us." So God will always be weak against us because he loves us.

We are of the race of Jacob. We are the true Israel, the one who fought the whole night long with the angel and deserved his name: "Strong against God."

How God speaks

There is a remarkable book with this romantic title: *God will speak this evening*. This title is in error, but the error is a very common one: God will not speak to us on any particular evening, he speaks to us all the time. He has always spoken to us in his own language, the austere and simple language of our daily life. We don't hear him because we would rather he spoke in our language, in the language of happiness as we understand it, in terms of impoverished and foolish satisfactions—emotion, vanity or even comfort—the only message that we have decided to recognize as his.

But God perseveres in speaking to us in his own language. God speaks to us in this language that we do not know and do not want to learn, he speaks to us of acceptance, of sacrifice, of renunciation, of his plan, so vast in scale, so unimaginably bold, so improbably generous, the plan by which he wills to save us, us and the world.

God speaks to us unceasingly through the events of our life, through the firmness with which he negates our petty human ordering of it, through the regularity with which he disappoints our plans and our attempts to escape, through his endless defeat of all our calculations by which we hoped to become able to do without him. And little by little he tames us, he draws us into relationship with him. Then one day, when we are helpless on a bed, stopped dead by some reverse, isolated by some misfortune, crushed by a sense of our own powerlessness, one day he brings us to the point of resigning ourselves to listening to his language, to admitting his presence, to recognizing his will.

And we realize then that he had always been speaking to us.

Poverty

In order to give, one must first consent to be poor. Shame on that man who wants to give without consenting to receive. One cannot give effectively or at depth unless one first recognizes one's own poverty, unless one feels solidarity with the distress one aims to relieve, stricken with the sickness of the person one aims to cure.

The man who desires to become poor begins by giving. But giving is still the act of one who is rich. To be poor means accepting that you have to receive and learning how to let yourself be enriched.

The poor man is perhaps he who is independent enough

of his own wealth to recognize that others have something to give him.

If any person, of whatever origin or worth, feels at ease in our company, feels himself to be conferring as much as he receives, that means we are truly poor.

A *Retreat*

During my holidays I attended an extraordinary retreat.

It was given by a parish priest who spoke of religion with the simplicity, freshness and naturalness with which you would speak to me about your job. He gave the same impression of security, sincerity and relaxation as an unbeliever. The religion he preached was completely stripped of sentimentality, brought heaven down to earth and God down in our fellow men.

It was a solidly materialistic religion, incarnate in history and living in time, with no spiritual evasions or pious alibis, a religion in which a man was judged by his acts and in which good intentions were no excuse for inefficiency, any more than fidelity to rites dispensed a man from truthfulness and honesty.

It was a retreat without pious exercises but at which we received all those human elements we need to be true Christians.

I'm telling you, it was an extraordinary retreat.

Contacts

To live means to establish real contact, easy communications with other people.

Man is, as it were, porous; he is designed for mutual interchange. He subsists only in virtue of his solidarity with his milieu. Breathing and feeding, for example, signify that the universe and we are of the same race, that we can assimilate it, that it can live in us and we in it. But there are other forms of interchange quite as natural and as necessary from which we cannot abstract ourselves save at the price of a sort of moral asphyxia or anorexia.

As soon as contact with others slows down or is broken off, there you have mental illness. It sometimes gives a curious impression of richness. "The man who has lost his reason," said Chesterton, "has lost everything except reason." The man who has lost contact has lost everything except himself. But what remains to him of himself? Depriving others of our wealth, deprives us of theirs. He who loses, gains. He who saves his soul, loses it.

The bond with others, which is love, is never absolutely self-centred or absolutely disinterested. It is a communication of life, a reciprocity of giving. As soon as anyone gives, the person who receives confers on him an even greater gift: he gives him the chance of giving. The man who gives, enriches. But he who knows how to receive, delivers. Your trust that opened the gate of your own soul, frees others from the prison of their individuality by allowing them to enter into you.

In order to be yourself you have need of the whole world. The soul of man is infinitely greater than one imagines. There is a modern novel in which the author describes a town visited by plague. It has to be surrounded and isolated by a *cordon sanitaire*. When the epidemic has drawn to its end, the gates are opened and the inhabitants are freed to take their first steps outside the city. And at that moment, out in the heather, out on the hills, they realize that they have all been suffering from an absence, from an exile that had no remedy, from a thirst that could never be slaked. That in order to be happy, in order to be themselves, even without moving from where they lived, they needed nothing less than the whole wide world around them, open and free; that in order to remain in peace, to breathe in peace within their little houses, they had to feel round about them the brotherly presence, the accessibility of all mankind.

Atheism

Are there any atheists? Some deny God with a vigour that suggests the power of his pressure on their minds; others seem, out of respect, to avoid defining what they believe in, for fear of distorting it.

But the true atheist is not the man who says that God does not exist. The authentic atheist hidden within each one of us is the one who affirms that God cannot change him, who denies that power of total transformation, that infinite power of creation and of resurrection that belongs to the Holy Spirit.

"Send forth your Spirit and they shall be created. And you shall renew the face of the earth," the Church proclaims every day in her incorrigible optimism.

The authentic atheist is the conservative, the one who asserts that, at his age (there are some who speak like this at the age of fifteen as at sixty), one doesn't change any more than one goes back to one's mother's womb, that he's too old, that he's too weak, that he's too hardened, that he's already tried and it's never worked, that nothing can be done with him.

How many there are among us like Nicodemus, how many doctors in Israel, who do not know that the spirit of love can bring a dead man back to life and even turn an ancient doctor back into a child!

Idleness

We are all very busy people. We all of us have a lot to do, too much to do. We no longer have the time to do nothing.

This means that we are delivered up whole and entire to our weakness, our moods, our cowardice.

Because we shall always find a thousand excuses for putting off or getting out of what we don't want to do. A heavy post allows us to select which letters we shall open first and, above all, which ones we shall answer straightaway, leaving on one side or else postponing, sometimes indefinitely, all the others. Motives will never be lacking, good ones at that, to dispense us from everything that bothers or scares us, for example, coming to a halt, reflecting, praying.

It is so much easier to let oneself go and just carry on working: "If I weren't so lazy," somebody once said, "I wouldn't work so much." That is why so many people take such a lot of trouble to fill up their holidays. If ever they had any spare time, perhaps they'd have to start thinking.

God is poor

God came into our world as a poor man. When he chose to reveal himself, when God came among us so that those who were his own might know him and he might know those who were his own, he came into the world as a poor man. He renounced, first of all, anything that could arouse interest, attract or impress: money, power. The state of life he chose was poor, his family were poor and the externals of their life were poor; and he did all this, not in order to hide himself away, that would be incomprehensible, nor to give a "good example," the idea is nauseating! but in order to manifest himself, in order to be known by us.

God is poor; he has nothing with which to reward those who love him. He is love; all he can do is to love. There is only one thing he can give—he can teach us to love as he does. He gives only the capacity to give. Who among us could endure the awful poverty, the terrible starkness of God? He is gift, he sets all his joy in an Other, all his heart on an Other, he keeps nothing for himself. He lives by giving. Those who love him must be alive with his love, "strong with his strength, rejoicing with his joy, because he has nothing else to give them." We are afraid of God. We mistrust his gifts. They are living gifts that work within those who receive them and bring them to pass them on in their turn; to become poor in imitation of the generosity and poverty of God, the two vices which a middle-of-the-road Christian cannot forgive.

The Humility of God

God is humble, not only in the commonplace logical sense that humility is truth and he knows himself in truth. God is humble in a far vaster and more lovely sense, in that he does not set his joy in himself, he cares nothing for his own glory, he attaches no importance to himself.

The Son does not speak of himself. He does nothing of himself, he knows nothing of himself, he knows only what he sees his Father doing. He who sees the Son sees not him but the one whom he tries with all his strength to reveal and to glorify, the Father.

The Father does not know himself, he does not love himself; only in his Son does he truly know and love himself, and every time he manifests himself, he shows to us an Other in whom he is more himself than in himself: that Son in whom he is well pleased.

And the Holy Spirit does not speak of himself, he says nothing of himself, he utters over and over again what he has learnt of an Other with the passion that springs of wonder and love.

Humility is needed not only for us to know man but also for us to know God. Humility sharpens our hunger for God because it is another name for love.

Acceptance

You long for love and with all your strength refuse it. This is because you always want to deserve the love people give you. You hate being loved gratuitously. But a love which is not gratuitous is not love; a love which does not love far beyond all motives for loving is mercenary, calculated, appraising, it is a response, not a gift. If you refuse the gift, you are refusing love, because love is gift.

And it is only by this gift that you will become worthy of love. Whatever there is of good in you will be awoken only by a love bold enough, gratuitous enough, that breaks through to it, awakens it and brings to birth in your heart a love as generous as itself.

Spring comes to the earth only because the earth consents to be loved in the state to which winter has brought her. Her only chance of blossoming again is to accept this help that is unhoped for, undeserved, and yet one in which she recognizes, far more than in the intervention of any other agent, the revelation of herself.

And the welcome, the acceptance you give to the generosity of others, the simplicity with which you believe them capable of loving you in this way, is the greatest gift that you can give them. They will realize the good they have within them for the sole reason that you allowed them to show it to you.

A man may think he loves his wife for a thousand and one little traits that are proper to her alone and endlessly fill him with pride, wonder and joy. But when he gets to love her better, he will realize that he loves her for reasons for which he could have loved any other woman. A husband, in the last analysis, is faithful to his wife for motives that would have kept him faithful to any other woman. It is just that no other woman could have aroused in him this total fidelity.

Parents think they love their children because they are theirs, because they belong to them, they are like them and because in them the parents see themselves. But their love will go through bitter moments of growth and deep renunciations, time and again it will have to transcend itself, and if they truly love their children, they will one day realize that they love them for motives for which they would have loved any child.

Contemplation

Christian contemplation is profoundly different from pagan contemplation.

A Christian does not become a contemplative in order to escape from the world, to go through spiritual experiences, to live by anticipation in the next world. The Christian contemplative contemplates an incarnate God, a crucified God, a saviour. It is therefore impossible to be a contemplative without becoming a missionary. Because it is impossible to know and love God without becoming like him.

St Teresa of the Child Jesus is the patron saint of the missions.

For us there is no question of inventing God, of journeying out to discover him in another world where he is hidden. Our task is to recognize him in this world where he manifests himself to those he loves. And those who do recognize him are always sent by him towards their brethren. He has always formed them after his own heart, he has made them missionaries.

Charles de Foucauld used to say that, for the sake of Christ's kingdom, he was ready to go to the ends of the earth and live to the end of the world. Precisely these are the dimensions of the missionary love of Christ: "Preach the Gospel to all nations," and "I am with you all days even to the consummation of the world."

Charles de Foucauld was a true contemplative; he had become a missionary like him whom he had contemplated.

"But I haven't done anything"

This is the excuse that gets a person thrown out of any good school and has the same effect in heaven.

The *Confiteor* is gravely incomplete; it accuses us of sinning only by thought, word and deed. It leaves out the principal sin, the sin of omission.

The last judgment, as described in the Gospel, terrifies those who think themselves just because they have done no evil.

The servant who kept his talent in perfect safety, beautifully wrapped up in a napkin, very clean—is stripped of it and condemned.

The wicked rich man had not robbed Lazarus. He had not treated him badly, had not even exploited him; he had just ignored him. His sin is the terrible one of not having seen him. Nor will he now see him for all eternity.

It was not the Levite or the priest who beat up the traveller on the way to Jericho and threw him bleeding into the ditch to lie there. They hadn't even given him the benefit of a sermon on his imprudence, nor had they taken advantage of his accident to reproach him for his impiety: "We told you so. You should have listened to us. . . ." All they did was to pretend they hadn't seen him. Their sin was the worst of all. They did nothing.

And when the good and the wicked are separated at the end of the world, the criterion, to everybody's great astonishment, will be this sin of omission: "You did not feed me, clothe me, visit me. . . ." "But, Lord, I didn't see you!"

That, precisely, is your sin.

Escapism

There is no other world. There exists only this world. God entered it and never left it.

It's no good trying to reach him in the next world. He is with us ever since the Word became flesh and chose to dwell among us.

Nothing is so hard for us to stomach as the Incarnation. The faithful are theists or spiritualists, but they are not Christians. They believe in the immortality of the soul but not in the immortality of the body. They believe that Jesus is God but neglect the fact that he is man. As far as they are concerned, in the words of the well-known hymn, "Earth has been visited by heaven," but the visit was one of compassion, not to say condolence, after which the visitor withdrew.

For us, heaven is on this earth. Christ is with us. "No man has ever known God," says St John. We know him only by knowing Jesus Christ, that is to say, God in a man.

Spiritualists long to leave this world. God enters it.

We want to cast off this heavy shroud of matter that weighs us down. But God became flesh and remained so. One can find him only in the flesh.

Spirituality is too often a sort of house-moving.

St Teresa of Lisieux wanted to spend her heaven in doing good on earth. What could be more natural, since heaven is here below? If Christ is living among us, how could she have wanted to be anywhere else?

Two Religions

Most people's religion boils down to what they do for God. When one speaks to them of God, what comes back to their memory is all that they have given up for him. Or else they get anxious and start worrying about what is going to be asked from them in his name. And since the things they have done for God, or that they are threatened with having to do, are in general gloomy, grudged and difficult, religion is for them something gloomy, impoverished and difficult. And because they don't want to have any more to do than they have done already, they don't want to know any more of religion than they know already, which is, as far as they are concerned, quite enough.

There is another sort of religion, absolutely different and the only true one, which consists in realizing and wondering at the things which God does for us. True religion does not lie in the gloomy, unsubstantial and impoverished things we do for God. That is natural religion. But our religion is supernatural. It speaks to us of the wonderful things, the unbelievable works that God, with such boldness of generosity and love, has done for us. One can never have enough of such a religion, one never tires of learning about it and of meditating on it. The true religion is one of joy and wonder and never ending thanksgiving for all that God does for us, for the great things that God can do in the lowliness of his servants.

Sinners

We are Christians not because we think ourselves better than other men nor because we are good-living, honourable men without reproach, but primarily because we recognize that we are sinners.

We are not Christians because we sit in the first places, but because we assign ourselves the last (with sincerity, not because we are counting on being led to the first. So many Christians who say the *Domine, non sum dignus* would be outraged to the depth of their souls if they were taken at their word and were refused communion. Humility is so well looked on that all put on a show of it. Genuine simplicity sometimes demands that we accept the armchair).

We are Christians because we sincerely believe we are not worth much.

Religion is full of terrible paradoxes. So many people think themselves no longer capable of being Christians because they are unchaste, weak and backsliding. But in fact there is a far greater number of people who will never be Christians because they think themselves just, honourable and pure.

Many Christians think themselves hypocrites and give up religion because they go on committing sins. They lose their faith after losing their morals. They think it is impossible to hold on to an exalted idea of God when they can no longer hold on to an exalted idea of themselves.

But I think that there is a far greater number of Christians alienated from religion without knowing it because they do not believe themselves to be sinners. (One asks oneself who is left after that!)

Because the redemption was not for the sake of the just but in order to seek out and save those who were lost. Those who are well have nothing to do with the doctor.

For the first Christians the Gospel was the Good News: God offered sinners his free forgiveness. For modern Christians the Gospel is bad news: they learn to their astonishment that they are sinners and that they need forgiveness.

We belong at Mass only if we recognize that we are sinners. The Mass is concerned only with sinners. It speaks either to them or for them in almost every one of its prayers. And yet the majority of the faithful present think of themselves as standing in some sort of golden mean. They tell themselves that they may have done nothing very good but then they have done nothing very bad either. Barricaded within a comforting mediocrity they keep each other warm.

But there is nothing very comforting about that position—the Lord's coming had nothing to do with any golden mean. A man who judges himself on such lines is automatically excluding himself from salvation.

How refreshing it would be if all the Christians at a Sunday Mass were to recognize that they are sinners and confess their unworthiness. What a relief from the huge and stifling hypocrisy that weighs upon us!

Jesus was happy to eat with sinners. But he could not endure the lies of the Pharisees.

I think that is one of the main reasons why people get so bored at Mass. We pretend to recognize that we are sinners and that this saddens us a bit. But in that case there is no escaping the corresponding pretence of being a bit happy because we have been forgiven. The Mass proceeds, the Mass is consumed between these two hypocrisies.

Joy lies in knowing oneself to be forgiven. The wonder is to discover that God is so much better than we are.

Because if God loved us by reason of our virtues, we

would forfeit his love by reason of our sins. But if his love is gratuitous, he will love us always. It is he who is good, not we. We will never have done with detachment from ourself and rejoicing in him.

Commit Christian Sins!

"Pone, Domine, custodiam ori meo, ut non declinat cor meum . . . ad excusandas excusationes in peccatis"—"Watch over my lips, O Lord, lest I cover up my sins with empty excuses."

The worst evil lies not in committing evil but in committing evil while pretending it is good.

Happy the man who commits evil knowingly. Woe to him who does evil and lies to himself.

It is better to commit a sin than to corrupt a principle.

It is better to sin with sincerity than to lie to oneself in order to stay virtuous.

You will repent of a straightforward sin more easily than of one wrapped in doubt. Don't muddy the water so as to fish from it whatever you desire, pretending all the while that it happened just by chance. Don't let yourself be paralysed with horror, disgust or simply deliberate inattention so as to be able thereafter to strike attitudes appropriate to a virgin martyr if someone takes you in his arms, because that is the idea you give to everybody while doing everything possible to hide it from your own conscience.

Don't unlock the door between your room and the next so as to let your neighbour come in should he want to, as you want him to, but without having to decide the thing yourself. It's not enough not to will evil. You must want there to be no evil.

Do not let the passage of time corrupt the situation and bring on a decision that you dare not take yourself.

It is better to do wrong and take responsibility for it than to let the responsibility drift. Because if you don't assume it, no more will you be able to discharge it.

Don't wait to find a good reason before you do evil because you will close down over yourself a sort of lid and you won't easily find other good reasons to remove it.

Don't take advantage of somebody else's mistake to give him a good impression, telling yourself that it can do no harm either to him or to you, because when he discovers his mistake, you will have lost your chance of giving him the only impression that should have been given: that of your honesty.

Do not lie by telling a half-truth, because the absence of the other half will make it look like a whole lie.

Commit straightforward, clear-cut and undeniable sins of which you will later be able to repent with the same sincerity you use in committing them—sins of avowed weakness and not sins of malice carefully arranged to look like anything (accident, distraction, pure chance, exception, services rendered, unforeseen situation, *force majeur*, even act of virtue) except sin.

The trouble is that in that case they can arouse any feeling (resentment, humiliation, spite, shame, disgust, despair, horror) except repentance.

If you are weak enough to sin, do not be too proud to recognize the fact.

Do not judge

How can one not judge? Does one have to stop thinking, feeling, appreciating? Every event, every situation, every personality provokes a judgment, and this isn't simply something spontaneous, something habitual or unavoidable; it is a duty.* Haven't I an obligation to choose, which means to judge, my friends, my books, my advisers, my colleagues, myself?

For it is too easy to pretend that the problem can be dismissed in the brief formula: judge acts, not persons. . . . What, after all, is an act, considered apart from a person? Isn't the important thing about an act the way in which it bears witness to a state? On many occasions, in any case, it is directly a person whom I have to judge. Whether it be those who ask me to judge them or to help them judge themselves, or whether it be myself.

The true sense of "do not judge" seems to me to be "do not condemn." You can and ought to evaluate acts and patterns of conduct, even intentions whenever you do in fact get to know them—you can even, though with infinite prudence, assess degrees of responsibility, but there is a limit beyond which you cannot go: you are forbidden to condemn, that is to say, forbidden to identify someone with his act, to consider him totally expressed by his behaviour in a given situation, to refuse him the benefit of any doubt that there might be more to him than this guilt, that he might regret it or atone for it.

A man is always worth more than any of his acts, more even than the sum of them. We all suffer from precisely this fatal disproportion between our soul and our life.

Take a person at the age of twenty and say to him: "I arrest you ['to stop' is the original and terrible sense of

* I am not including here the case of the judge, which is entirely different in that from him we demand not a moral but merely a social judgment. He does not pronounce on a man's responsibility in conscience, but on the application of the law, designed for the defence of society. A legal code should find its inspiration in morality without pretending to be an exact reflection of it. It is a conventional compromise between morality and the facts of social life.

the legal term]; I am going to judge you: here is the good and here the evil that you have done; their totals and the difference between them make up you, that's what you're worth, that's what you are."

He is certain to answer: "That's not true, I am not the person you say I am. Fair enough, your sums are right; the injustice lies elsewhere. Nothing of what is truly me appears in your inventory. My deepest and truest self has always been on the point of expressing itself and has always been prevented. . . . I was positive that one day, next year, in spring, tomorrow, I would get the chance to start the sort of life I really want, to become the man I really am, the person that all my actions bear witness to but don't express."

Arrest him at the age of thirty, at the age of forty, and he will tell you the same: "I haven't yet been able to realize what's in my heart. I am still waiting for the occasion, the person, the milieu, the circumstances in which I shall at last be able to be myself and act in accordance with my true nature."

Arrest him at the age of sixty, he will protest the same. At 100 he will be simultaneously more resigned to your verdict, because so discouraged, and more certain than ever that you have missed the essential. And far from considering himself responsible for this disproportion between what he is and what he has done, he laments it, he is its victim, and he reckons it virtue in himself to endure it with patience.

A patriarch who lived more than 700 years left behind him this short testimony: "The days of my life have been brief and evil." He hadn't had time, he hadn't had the chance, to say what he really thought, to do what he would have liked to do. His life remained at a terrible remove from his intentions.

Newman said that he had often thought this at the deathbed of friends: that nobody had really known them, that nobody had loved them as they should have been loved. Even if they had held high office, enjoyed great influence, left behind them some great work and many disciples, the best that lay within them had not been known.

The greater they were, the more timid, even adolescent, they had remained in the presence of life and the less they had been able to disclose of what was deepest and most intimate in their mind and character, and those who loved them best had been able to do no more than guess at all these things.

There is always an immeasurable distance between a man and his acts. These express him in the sense that an artist's works express without exhausting what he is trying to convey, and even as he creates them, he rejects them. Nothing less than all eternity is needed for the flowering of a living soul. The worst wrong that one can do it is to deny the infinite possibilities that it contains, to confuse it with and reduce it to its present or its past, to make of it something dead and unchangeable, something that can be manipulated and utilized–an object.

There is a sort of satanic satisfaction to be found in "classing" a person, in identifying him once and, as we hope, for all with his outward seeming, in reducing him to a single aspect of his character. It's convenient. I've got rid of him. He no longer exists for me. It's as if I had killed him. I have killed him.

And that perhaps is what lies behind the extraordinary promise, "And you will not be judged." If others remain for you living persons, if your sympathy for them is shown by what you expect from them, by the attention and respect you give them (that sort of tireless passionate interpellation that speaks most powerfully to their most inward depths), then you too are still living. From you who expect new things from others there is still something new to be expected. You must not be condemned, treated as a thing, cut off like so much dead wood that is fit only for burning. You are still part of the vine. The fact that you set yourself on a branch full of life, that you affirm, appreciate and cherish the existence round about you of so many branches running full with sap, is the sign that you yourself are still living.

"Union differentiates"

TEILHARD DE CHARDIN

"I need to be alone in order to be myself; I want to protect my originality, to push my individuality to the limit; I want to discover my own depths and contemplate the depths of all things. I can only appreciate myself in solitude. I am only fully myself if no other person comes to distract me, to appeal to those capacities I have for communion with others, that dissolve my essential self. And the sadness that I sometimes feel intensifies my experience of my own personality."

And yet the harshest punishment that can be inflicted on a man is to shut him up alone with himself. Hell is a state of total excommunication. Christ feared neither men nor suffering but he feared solitude: "You are going to leave me alone. You have not been able to watch one hour with me. My God, my God, why have you abandoned me?"

I need others in order to be myself. In God the divine nature is such as to demand three divine persons. Man was created in the image of God: he was made male and female, he was made plural. The presence of others, the action of others, is for him the best possible approach to his own most intimate secret: he is capable of loving.

It is in this that we are God's image, not in our intelligence or free will or the cold fact of our being spiritual creatures. The Lord's command is not: Be rational as God is rational ("Man is a rational animal"), but: Be merciful as God is merciful; turn towards others with love.

Man was created incapable of self-sufficiency, incapable of successfully turning in upon himself. He is made to give himself and to receive, to find in another his complement and to set his heart upon another. He knows himself better, he loves himself better in another, and the wonder of it awakes in him the noblest resources of his being. "The communion of one person with another can take place only over their own heads, in virtue of that movement by which each one of them, no longer thinking of himself but solely of the other so as to help summon him to a higher form of life, thereby receives from him that life which he longed to give him" (Lavelle).

Knowledge is a sort of unfolding of oneself (*Intellectus fit quodammodo omnia*). To know another means that I have already become more myself. But loving him means living in him more than in me, it means living more because more than once. It's perfectly true that there is a form of association with another that can oppress, alienate, stifle, depersonalize. But there are others which exalt a man and cause the flowering of his whole personality. Anyone who has spent his life in true friendship knows that nothing made him so keenly experience how rich he was and how alive as the presence of others.

The highest form of self-possession is the capacity to give oneself; it is not an avarice that holds one captive of one's own possession.

A communal soul is being awakened within mankind; a planetary sensitivity, a world awareness, an appetite for knowledge on the scale of the universe. The same thought, the same feeling, the same invention occur simultaneously at several different points on the earth.

The most violent and the most neglected passion of mankind is the passion for the universal. Once we have grasped what is just, what is true, what is good, with the full intensity of this passion, nothing thereafter can call a halt to the intractable violence of our quest. Perhaps the only motive force capable of mobilizing the dormant or wasted energy of mankind is a world patriotism.

Bigots

Bigots and libertines are in agreement on their first premiss; only the way they apply it distinguishes them. For both of them religion is the enemy of life, nature is opposed to grace and God cannot be reconciled with joy. Nothing religious can be anything but unpleasant. So bigots live without pleasure an unpleasant life which assures they go to heaven. At least they think so. The others, preferring a pleasant life here and now (a bird in the hand is worth two in the bush) are resigned to living as pagans and philosophically renounce their chance of heaven. (The danger of meeting there only the pious folk abovementioned makes the loss in any case not too difficult to contemplate.)

But it is the same God who creates and redeems. The saints, after long striving, rediscover what nature really is. On every page of the Gospel Christ observes it, rejoices in it, speaks of it and praises it. The opening of his mission is flooded with joy. Paradise is found again. God manifests himself on the same level as our interests. He delights fishermen with the gift of fish, the crowds with a gift of bread, drinkers with wine, the sick with healing, the poor with good tidings. He scandalizes the Pharisees, the bigots of his time, who call him a glutton and a wine drinker.

God reveals himself in the deepest joy before he reveals himself in the greatest love.

What we really want always happens to us

A man's deepest will is always effective. God really has placed man in the power of his own decision. So many astonishing events seem to prove that a constant will infallibly attains its purpose. A child will say as he contemplates the result of his actions: "I never intended that." But a man will recognize his responsibility for his own destiny.

"The achievements of adult life," said Barrès, "are always the effect of some great thought of youth." We shall live what we have dreamed. We shall attain everything we willed. That's why most men attain nothing. They don't know what they want. They want nothing.

With a little faith one moves mountains. There is nothing hidden that will not be revealed, there is nothing secret that will not be known. What you murmured in hidden places, on your pillow as you dreamt, will be preached on the rooftops.

We shall need no other judgment than our lives. What we have wanted will be made plain by where we have got to. Hell will be paved with our intentions, fictitious or unrealized, but heaven will blaze with acts. The true life of a man has no element of chance in it. Whatever happens to him, resembles him.

A symptom worth thinking about is this: Would any

man like to exchange his lot for another's? What I have in mind is not change of health, fortune, physique, abilities or wife but a change of "I," an exchange of life. Nobody would.

Those who say they would, do so because they fail to reflect, they don't know themselves, they don't imagine the other. What they would like is to be simultaneously the other and themselves. But to be only the other? No!

If this is true it proves that we are, each one of us, what we want to be, that we all hold on with passionate intensity to our own personality and that, in spite of anything we might say to the contrary, nothing could be harder for us than to change from what we are.

One can say something true only by saying something new

One can say something true only by saying something new. Whenever a really living word gives an answer to problems and lights up a situation, we all of us feel that it must have been shaped specially for and at that moment. Only what I grasp for the first time is absolutely true.

Truth, like man, is invented anew every moment. A truth repeated is a dead truth, one that has become an object, something that can be transmitted but no longer gives life because it no longer has life.

Ideas grow old and die as men do, but faster. Take the most brilliantly formulated, the most striking idea that springs from us when a keen awareness and the right moment conspire together; once the time is past when to expound it is to develop and feed it, to discover all its blessed fruitfulness, once I am simply repeating it and trying to recapture the warmth it communicated when new and spontaneous, then from that moment onward the thought is frozen, gets distorted, extinguished, incapable of shedding new light on the situation for whose sake I bring it out again.

Truth is not an object. It is a relationship of man to world and of man to man. And nothing changes faster than men. A man is never twice the same; neither then is his truth.

Truth is as changeable, as shifting, as personal as men are or should be. And when it fails them or when it fails itself by becoming frozen into an object, it makes them like itself and they die as they accept it.

"If one thinks literally today as men did 500 years ago, one cannot escape thinking in a different spirit" (Blondel, *Lettre sur les Exigences*).

"Let us seek as if we were bound to find, and let us find with the intention of never ending our search" (St Augustine).

"Nobody comes closer to knowledge of the truth concerning the divine than he who understands that, even were he to advance very far, there still remains further ground to cover. For the man who imagines he has reached his goal has not found what he sought but has faltered in his quest" (St Leo).

A *Face*

The greatest love that one can show a person is to reveal to him a countenance of himself, one in which he can recognize and accept himself.

We do not know who we are, we are absent from ourselves, restless, bitter and unhappy. That is why each one of us wears a mask that protects and reassures us, lets us take a place in the company of all other mask wearers. We are hasty in choosing it, and one follows another as dictated by the latest novel, the latest film, the lastest mask we met.

Where is the man of humility or insolence enough to dare walk round without a mask?

Or, rather, who will love us enough, who will show us the respect and the tenderness needed to encourage us to lay our mask aside? Aggressive, cold, violent, distant, indifferent or pitiful—so many masks and all of them ludicrous, with which we conceal our wretchedness or emptiness—such patience and gentleness, such a power of persuasion is needed to bring us to cast them away. Much more will be needed—a sort of genius, a blend of divination and creation—to bring into existence the face which was ours but which we would never have been able to clear for ourselves and in which, when presented to us, we can at last recognize and accept ourselves.

Old Age

Have you ever visited an old folks' home? How rare it is to find a person who ages well! Why do the faculties deteriorate as age and experience increase? Why does life grow so impoverished as it draws to its climax? Intelligence, memory, imagination—all right, but interest in others, the gift of sympathy, generosity, love, why do they vanish to make way for that fearful self-centredness of the old, who refer all things to themselves? And, in that very act, grow absent from themselves. One still respects them as one respects unused churches. Our feelings make us smile to them as to children but with a heart secretly petrified with dread at their decline.

And how swiftly old age comes! That person is old who becomes incapable of understanding something he hasn't understood before, who listens only in order to catch those ideas he has already, who ceases to invent his own life or to take any part in the inventing done by others. How many old people there are! And yet life is renewal and creation—it should not be a sort of collapse. There are old people who make a discovery, an exploration of old age, who are not content with the memory of what went before but whose horizon grows broader as their life contracts. Ought not a true old age to be a new light that shows up quite differently all that one hitherto had thought one had seen and understood?

When the fountain of life in a man springs up too violently, it blinds and deafens. "His youth makes too great a noise in his ears; he can hear nothing," said Madame de Sévigné of her twenty-year-old son. Youth is inexperienced, harsh, inflexible, hasty. It has no patience with the long waits demanded by contemplation. It loses the present in its greed for the future. In the pride of its strength it disregards the help of others and the beauty of the world. With age, life slows down enough to let a person look round, open out, be enriched by all those lives which could find no access to us save through our more peaceful possession of our own life.

Prayer

I don't like the common assertion that beginners in the religious life are drawn along by God with sensible effects of grace. I think that such effects are those of nature itself, hungering for God after long deprivation of him and after wearying of all else.

Later, in the long run, it can happen, not that nature grows tired of him but that it feels the awakening of other longings, calls back memories of pleasures made more vivid by austerity, or simply experiences the dead weight of faculties deliberately frustrated without any of the objects designed for them.

There is certainly something very attractive in the patristic saying that the experience of spiritual joy is the reverse of that of temporal: when without it, one does not desire it; but once having tasted it, one desires it more and more.

But it seems to me that our nature hungers for God even when it broke with him long ago, perhaps the more intensely the longer ago it was. It experiences a sort of famine. But the devil rides it and spurs it on, to distract it from its own need. He changes its hunger into haste. That is why people today are in such a hurry. Their speed is to distract their hunger. A man may not know where he is going, but he's going there fast. The dizziness of hunger is confused with the intoxication of the race.

If they call themselves Christians, they bargain ferociously over the few moments which they concede to God. And then, they don't know what to do with the moments that they have saved from him, and they throw them to the dogs.

But let them find themselves for one moment in God's presence, and they know at once what it was they were looking for in such a way as never to find it.

In prayer, time lasts, acquires a character, is tasted. Elsewhere it is broken into fragments, it merely evaporates; however much one consumes, it has neither taste nor consistency. One drinks it without thirst.

Whereas in prayer it acquires a density such that a given instant becomes sufficient to itself; there is no desire for it to pass, one would like only to prolong it. Time is conquered, haste is no more. The creature is restored to the natural flow of its spirits. It is God who bears up his creature, not his creature that forces itself onward. At last it is living at the very rhythm of its creation.

The Stages of the Redemption

The promise of salvation is as "original" as sin, and the story of that sin and the proclamation of its punishment outline the programme of the redemption. God does not simply promise his forgiveness and, in a certain sense, take revenge on the tempter; he spells out the consequences of the sin and, by that same token, lays down the stages of its reparation.

We are to be, with God, in subordination to his action but in co-operation with him, the instruments of this great work.

The Redeemer will be born of a woman. The redemption that began with the consent given by her alone among us, will be brought to its completion with the collaboration of us all. Its effects will grow and broaden out down the centuries. The forgiveness of original sin will be the beginning of and the means to the alleviation of its penalties. Little by little man will recover the ground lost by sin.

Man will retain the animals, retain the soil. The invention of machinery will lighten his toil and make of it once more a human and a happy activity as when he was in Paradise and kept and cultivated it and "named" the animals. Obedience to grace will always be followed by an advance of nature, and every disobedience will be paid for by a regression, by our becoming subject to that very thing which we had invented in order to achieve our liberty.

For woman, the distress of childbearing will be lessened. She will progress towards a childbearing that is easy, voluntary and spiritualized, on the model of that which was granted first of all to Our Lady. Her children will save her from herself (I Tim. 2.15) and will give her a balance of which her nature frequently deprived her.

Her relationship with man will be transformed also: not only will he cease, swiftly in practice, slowly in law and right, to dominate her, but that unhappy cleft made between man and woman by sin will be superseded as the union is restored to its original state; they will be two in one flesh (Matt. 19.6-8). The sacrament of marriage will make them equal and inseparable and one day persevering fidelity to the promises and demands of baptism will take away every form of separation, subordination, inequality: "There will no longer be either Jew or Greek, slave or free, man or woman" (Gal. 3.28).

The present inferior status of woman, her exclusion, for example, from the priesthood, is not an inevitable consequence of her nature but is the work of sin which must, by both man and woman, be progressively eliminated.

The tree of life, from which a single sin banished us for ever, will be replaced by a Living Bread that will confer immortality on all those (*pauper, servus et humilis*) whose sole entitlement will be the endless renewal of their repentance and God's forgiveness.

We shall recover the longevity of the patriarchs—that signifies little, but we shall one day attain the immortality that was Adam's. Why should old age be inevitable and irreversible? Those who believe in Christ will never see death, will not return to the earth.

The division of mankind at the Tower of Babel will be abolished; men will speak to one another in the universal tongue of charity, and a planetary patriotism will launch them at last upon their true mission: the conquest of the universe.

Felix culpa! A far higher order will replace the first. Even as Christ surpasses Adam, and Mary, Eve, so does the generosity of God's forgiveness surpass that of his primal gift, so does the order of redemption established for ever surpass that of the earthly paradise and will do so ever more and more. "O God, who most marvellously created the dignity of human nature and still more marvellously restored it. . . ."

The Vocation of St Peter

The vocation of St Peter consisted in this: once he knew the Lord, he knew himself; he recognized that he was nothing but a sinner and that his vocation was endlessly to measure his personal insignificance against the power and the glory of God.

Until he met Jesus, Peter thought he was somebody, he thought there was quite a lot he could do, he had a certain confidence in his own powers. But the passing of the Lord left him stripped of all self-love. The best preparation for his dignity as supreme head of the Church was the revelation of his incompetence, his total powerlessness and colossal weakness. He, so impetuous, so sure of himself, so swift to assume responsibility and speak his mind, reached the point of begging the Lord to withdraw from him, to abandon him, he saw that he was unworthy, he was emptied of all presumption and self-sufficiency, he was reduced to zero.

It is perfectly true that he was going to need many more trials, disappointments and failures before he fully learnt that lesson; he would forget again, he would make, as we all do, desperate efforts endlessly to take back what we have given, to deny what we have learnt, to attempt to get by on our own efforts.

But God perseveres, God is faithful. He was going to fulfil in Peter all he had promised him from that first encounter by the Lake of Genesareth. God was going to renew his light and his grace, and one day Peter, completely emptied of self, ardent as no other in his repentance and love, was going to say to him, so humbly, so sadly: "Lord, you know everything, you know well that I love you."

Everything began on the lakeside on that morning when the Lord borrowed Peter's boat because the people were pressing forward too vigorously to listen to him. While the Lord spoke, Peter listened to him with admiration and perhaps with a certain pride at the things being spoken in his boat. And if I may dare go on inventing (after all the imagination sometimes is the only thing creative enough to discover the truth), Peter listened to the Lord with, deep down in his heart, a certain awareness of himself, a certain confidence in himself. Peter had his own skills, his own worth: he could fish. The Lord spoke and spoke well, spoke as no man had ever spoken. But as for Peter, speaking wasn't his business. He appreciated sermons and could get a lot of pleasure from a good preacher. But his job was fishing, and he was good at his job.

Then, when he had finished speaking, the Lord turned towards Peter and said to him: "Now, Peter, let us go fishing." Peter was surprised as if his thoughts had been read. "It's no good," he answered him, "we've been working a whole night through without catching anything." "Let's go nonetheless," said Jesus. And the miracle happened by which Peter was utterly overcome.

There, at his own game, on his own ground, so to say, Jesus had beaten him and had revealed to him that he needed the Lord, that he was nothing without the Lord even at things at which he thought he excelled. Peter was converted, not by a sermon, but by a catch of fish. Jesus cornered him in his last stronghold, emptied him of his last self-satisfaction, forced him to confess that before him he was as nothing.

That is how every genuine Christian vocation begins. At certain moments religion ceases to be a luxury, a proof of our good education, an index of our culture. Quite suddenly we realize that to fulfil even our most ordinary duties, to love our wife or our husband, even to accept this child or that, we need prayer, we need help, we need God. On such days we discover that we are separated from shame, scandal and folly by a thread so slender that only a miracle saves it from breaking. Just as St Peter learned that it needed nothing less than a miracle for him simply to be able to fish, we know that if we remain a good man or a good woman, it is by an overwhelming grace beyond all understanding which makes us cry out to God with wonder from the depths of our unworthiness.

The Imagination

The master faculty of the mind is the imagination. One never says anything true except when saying something new. If you say something absolutely true, everyone will think that it is new. Even to see correctly, the imagination is needed, we have to give ourselves an account (and then check it) of what there is to see. Reality has an odd way of always being a little feeble, a little below what it ought to be. Creative genius perfects that which is, in the same way that Adam perfected God's creation by giving names to living creatures. To name a creature is to give it a further dimension of existence, to assert how we see it and teach others how it should be seen. The world is unfinished. Life becomes living only if there is a being to read the sense of its purposes and fulfil its longings.

When we attend with maximum intensity to another person, we reach a point at which we no longer see him, no longer listen to his words, no longer remember who he is but, placing ourselves absolutely at his disposal, we open ourselves to what he could be. The really moving thing in the work of education is listening to a person at the deepest level while preserving round all that he confides us of himself a halo of mystery, patience, care and love, thanks to which, sometimes, we can free him from what he is and give him access to his future.

The true service we have to render him is not knowing him but inventing him. No knowledge is of any value unless it is vivified by such love and attention that it becomes creative.

Difficult Children

"A man had two sons. He spoke to the first, saying: 'My son, go and work today in my vineyard.' He replied: 'I will not.' But subsequently he repented and went there. Then the man spoke to the second son and gave him the same order. He answered him: 'I will go, lord.' But he did not. Which of the two did his father's will?"

The whole drama of adolescence is in this parable. No long commentaries are needed on the docile child, the "mother's darling," sweet, soft, saying yes to everything, who has no doubts and who thereby shows up the weakness, the lack of reflection, the wretched dependence that will keep him everlastingly a child.

But do you understand, do you really prefer the first? Did you recognize your son in that insolent reply: "I will not." Ah! How we must love that difficult child, racked and excruciated by his need of independence. He is pessimistic, he knows how weak he is, he lacks confidence in his own strength, he thinks so ill of himself! And perhaps it is because his conscience is too fine, because he once failed to keep his word, that he no longer dares ever to give it. Or perhaps it is you that have treated him badly, repressed him, you may have made him lose confidence by refusing him yours. But there is an even better explanation of his revolt. Your son is too kind, too soft-hearted, too sensitive, he wants too much to please you, he tends too much to yield to you. He feels that this is not right. So he must first of all say no, affirm his independence, show clearly that it is not from weakness, childishness or sentimentality that he obeys, so that he may thereafter, with liberty, free both of himself and of you, of his fear and of his servile attachment, give an authentic love and obedience.

Two Illusions

We are never as good as we imagine, but we are rarely as bad as we begin to think at our first moments of self-knowledge. Whoever undertakes the task of learning to know himself goes on a terrible voyage from which he returns pale and stricken but ready for all the tasks that life may set him.

He has learnt that it is our vices that invariably provide the greatest motive force to our virtues. Never does one do good so cheerfully as when one does it for bad reasons. And how many fine and splendid causes there are in whose name we do evil, gorging the monsters in the dark places of our soul while our face is upturned towards the stars!

If we were to analyse the motives of our highest enterprises, we would be horrified. Fénelon, so noble, so religious, used to say that when he looked into himself he thought he saw reptiles. (A worlding? An intriguer? An actor?)

A monk observed that every time the sun shone and nature looked beautiful he found excellent reasons for visiting his sick friends; visiting those in distress is a work of mercy; we must hand on to men what we receive from God and be able to sacrifice our own peace to their comforting. At other times there was a change of key. How disedifying it is, he used to say to himself, to see monks rushing all over the place in spite of their vow of stability; the redemption of the world is wrought in prayer, not in agitation; the monk's cell is his true battlefield. But this was always when it was raining.

A man enters a seminary in order to convert the world but remains there when he has understood that it would already be a great deal to convert himself. Sometimes, aghast at discovering the motives for which he undertook the noblest enterprises, he is tempted to give up everything and to proclaim our baseness by renouncing our edifying lies.

But I think that this is another illusion. Our motives are often no more than the outward clothing of our conduct. They are like parasites that cover and ceaselessly gnaw at the substance of our moral life. But that substance is very different from all the pictures we form of it and, suitably stripped down, would perhaps look far more like the ideal that torments us and that we despair of serving, than the base instincts that come and feed upon it.

The Modern Rosary

Most of us seem to experience the greatest difficulty in being faithful to prayer. People find it incredibly difficult to pray. We are incapable of staying quietly in God's presence. We cannot endure the silence and stillness that alone could give us access to him.

In God's presence we are like those young people who need a radio as background while they study for their exams. Many modern children are so absent-minded, nervous and excitable that the music of a radio is an aid to work instead of a distraction. If it were not for the rosary of sounds which, slipping past bead by bead as it were, keeps up their concentration, sustains them and establishes some sort of peace-creating presence in their poor empty souls, they would suffer from such an emotional vacuum, such an inner poverty, that they would get up, run to the window, go down to the drawing-room or the kitchen looking for someone to talk to. Warmly suckled on noise, like well-fed babies, they become capable of staying still.

I think that this is how things stand with prayer for the majority of modern men and women. They are simply incapable of praying for five minutes in a row, not because they don't want to, on the contrary, they would like to pray, but because they are incapable of concentration, cannot endure silence, cannot stay in one place, cannot wait and listen. An ungovernable nervous energy drives us on, rushes us into some urgent piece of work, some errand that has to be run, some service that has to be rendered—it doesn't matter what, provided it means movement, action, talking, escape. Just think: we narrowly escaped a conversation with God! We very nearly had to stop telling lies, fussing, worrying, we very nearly had to fall silent and put ourselves into the hands of another, very nearly had to accept release from that burden against which we curse unceasingly but hold on to more firmly than life itself.

In that case, since we have such an aversion to prayer, since our education in this field hasn't even begun, why not make a humble beginning by going up to God without even trying at first either to speak to him or listen to him; why not simply put ourselves in his presence—and as standing still before him so terrifies us, why not begin by living, with complete naturalness, long moments at his side? Let's provide ourselves with a mental equivalent of the radio or a rosary, a novel, some knitting, whatever. Is there anything disrespectful in going to read a book in church? If your father or your wife is alone in the drawing-room and you go downstairs to read in their company, are they pleased or offended? And doesn't the quality of anything we do change completely according to the company in which we do it?

I think that, for modern people to be tamed for the Lord, they must be able to share with him at least one of their normal occupations. Little by little they will get a taste for his presence and come to the point one day of preferring the Lord to their reading. Like the child who plays in his mother's company, without speaking to her, without looking at her, without turning to her, with barely a moment's distraction from his playing. But take away his mother and he will realize that the whole joy of his playing was due to her presence and that he was in deepest contact with her precisely when saying nothing, asking for nothing, in a peaceful and loving silence—the sort of contact we should have when we pray.

The Handmaid to whom all Grace was given

Devotion to Our Lady is a sore spot nowadays in Christian spirituality. It ought to be impossible to love the Father and not to love Mary. She too can say to us: "If God were your Father you would love me because it is from God that I come."

And it should not be possible to love Mary and not to love the Father!

Alas, these two impossibilities are realized every day and all with any degree of responsibility for the religious life should be making every effort to eliminate these two dangers.

One is obviously graver than the other; there can be no worse terror than not knowing the Father, not praying to the Father, not loving the Father. How many Christians actually believe that the Father himself loves us? And this is also the more natural danger to fall into since man finds it easier to attach himself to the creature without rising to the Creator than he does to do the reverse.

That is why one should speak of Mary only with prudence and discretion. At a time when the central themes of religion are in such oblivion, when our Masses are dead, our sacraments like sealed books and the Scriptures for the most part unknown, it would be a good idea to have a genuinely Holy Year dedicated to the Mass, the Bible, the Liturgy, or even simply to the honour of the Father, to the knowledge of the Son and the preaching of the Holy Spirit. When you consider, for example, how "among us Catholicism is dying the death of Sunday Mass boredom," and this fifty years after Pope Pius X declared that "active participation by the faithful in the sacred Mystery is the primary and indispensable condition of the authentic Christian spirit," you might think it more urgent and in any case more useful to devote a year to explaining, to arousing and to promoting within the Church the "priesthood" of the laity.

Only too often devotion to Our Lady and the saints flourishes in direct proportion to the de-Christianization of the people. All those who find God too distant, Christ too divine, revelation insufficient, the Holy Spirit ineffective, seize upon secondary devotions, dubious apparitions and private revelation. The periphery fills up as the centre grows empty. The price of exalting human intermediaries is, only too often, a corresponding impoverishment of people's image of God. All those who consider that God did not sufficiently reveal himself in Christ, that God did not come sufficiently close to us in Christ, that God did not show us favour enough in Christ—all these are ripe for the coming of Antichrist.

It is hateful to think of Our Lady reduced to the object of such a devotion, reduced to being the focus of such an expectation. She who received from God everything that she gives us, sees her faithless and unhappy subjects abstract from God whatever good they think of or expect from herself or the saints.

As if anyone could show us greater goodness than the Father, as if anyone could better love the world than he who gave his only Son to save it, as if any creature could understand us better than our Creator does.

Those who love Mary should take jealous care to point out in her all that God does for his creatures, all that he is ready to do for everyone that opens himself to him, all that he was able to do in the only creature that ever did open herself to him. Nobody's devotion to Mary can grow to its full stature if he does not rejoice in her at the great things that God has done in the lowliness of his handmaid.

Limbo

In the imagination of many Christians and of some theologians, the sacraments instituted to give access to salvation have effectively denied it to every child that dies without baptism. A too material understanding of the sacraments has led them to think that to be deprived of baptism, the sole normal means of incorporation into Christ, meant the damnation of those denied the benefit of it.

Under the dispensation of the Old Testament, the just were saved by their faith, and children dying before the age of reason were justified by the faith of their parents. How could the dispensation of grace, established by Jesus Christ, "who desires the salvation of all men," render salvation more difficult or even, one should say, exclude from salvation children who did not refuse it?

All theologians admit that God can save children that die unbaptized by an act of grace which they term "extraordinary," because it is performed outside the framework of those means by which grace is normally given, even though there could be no act more natural and more normal for a God who "desires that not one of his little ones should be lost."

Such teaching is not only a consolation for parents who have lost a child before its baptism. It is of real importance that they should know that their prayers, their blessing and the offering up of their sorrow can constitute a baptism for him. Because these acts express their faith as baptism would have done, they are appealing to God in the most irresistible way. Instead of discouraging such parents by forcing them to believe that their children will be for all eternity separated from them, the Church should teach them, on the contrary, to surrender their children with unconditional trust into the hands of the Father.

The Religion of Absence

The distinguishing mark of the religion of many of our contemporaries is this: it is the religion of God's absence.

Present day religious life lacks confidence and enthusiasm (The Greek *en theo* means "in God").

Our Catholic writers in any case are happy only with mourning, lamentation and despair. The whole of modern Catholic literature bears witness to the absence of God.

This is very frequently what we even make our faith and our merit consist of: with deep respect we keep his place empty, we, unlike other men, abstain from filling it with idols, pleasures and distractions. We live in expectation of an epiphany that never happens. We long for a presence.

Nothing could be more contrary to authentic Christianity. Our religion is the religion of the presence of God. The religion of his Incarnation, of his *real* presence.

Jesus gave us his own word for it: "I will come to you, you will know me, I will not leave you orphans!" Orphans—that is absolutely the word that sums up the religion of most of our modern faithful. God seems scandalously absent and inactive. Our children do not produce many objections against the faith but they do have one, generally latent, of which all the others are simply expressions: what reality has all this?

But the apostles never complained of the absence of Jesus. On the contrary, it is from the moment at which he became invisible that their certitude, unfailing joy and spiritual confidence must be dated. No, they did not regret the time when Jesus was visible among them. They felt themselves to be filled with him, overflowing with him, infectious with his presence. Wherever they went they bore witness of God's presence and the working of his power. St Paul proudly uttered these words which shock us: "If once I knew Jesus according to the flesh, now I no longer know him according to the flesh" (II Cor. 5.16).

All this wealth is lacking in our Christians. They are sad as if they had been forsaken. They are in doubt both of God and of themselves. They certainly can no longer be compared to fountains springing up—the Holy Spirit seeps slowly within them instead of springing up into life everlasting.

And the reason for this is always the same: Individualism has led us to seek for God within ourselves. And he exists only in others by which I mean, in the love which we bear one to another.

The desire of Christ is not to unite us to himself alone but to unite all to each other: "Let them be one." He is never living in the life of anyone who seeks him while excluding others. But he lives with unbelievable intensity wherever two or three are united in his name. All who have ever lived with others in a union of authentic brotherhood know the joy and the faith which springs from it. Our faith, and above all our children's faith, depends primarily on the existence of a Christian community that is happy, affectionate and fervent, a community to which we can attach ourselves.

The absence of God in our life is perhaps only the absence of our brethren.

"These attempts of various kinds and varying worth, these unsupervised acts of initiative whose purpose is to make the liturgy come alive, bring religion down to the level of the faithful and appeal to the emotions instead of to faith."

If you want to raise people's level, ought you not to take them as they are, speak to them in words they understand, so as to lead them where you think they ought to be? To bring them to make an act of faith is all very well. But they still should know what their act of faith is in. The liturgy is designed to arouse and direct the act of faith. Otherwise you might as well be making one before a blank wall.

I went to daily Mass for all of the six years I spent at college, making acts of faith—but they were in the real Presence, the only thing I had understood about the Mass, the only thing I was taught to see in it; and I concentrated on the Host that was offered to my eyes at the Consecration, to my mouth at the Communion (and this with an unceasing regret that I could not touch it as the priest did, so much was the Host itself the object proposed to our faith).

It took me years of reading before I achieved, as if by chance, some understanding of our participation in the death and resurrection of Christ, in his obedience and exaltation, before I learned to value the "great" elevation less than the "little" elevation, to consider the *Amen* as a ratification of the Canon and not as an introduction to the *Pater*, to realize that the Offertory is not an offertory but a doublet of the Canon and that the Communion is not a "private communion" but an incorporation into my brethren, in short, to straighten out all the twisted acts of faith to which a dead liturgy had left me prey.

"But the function of the liturgy is not, as you seem to imply, to explain, to express the mystery. It is quite as much to veil it. In every religion there is a respect for the sacred, a sense of awe in the presence of the unknown."

You are 100 per cent mistaken. The Christian religion is the revelation of the mystery and, mark this well, the more the mystery is known, the more it is mystery. To veil the mystery leads simply to ignorance of it, and what a blasphemy it would be to think it would be more sacred in virtue of being less known. The more you proclaim the mystery, as St Paul did, the more you will lead men to wonder at the greatness of God. As things are, you have veiled it so effectively that what you get is apathy. God is word, gift, self-revelation, and you have made him into a silence, a sphinx, into gibberish!

Latin

There still exists, if you can believe it, supporters of Latin in the liturgy.

"The employment of this sacred language is more fitting," they say, "to the sanctity of the sacraments and divine worship. It promotes in the faithful the sense of mystery."

Are you not confusing the Christian mystery with the merely mysterious? The mystery is a truth too rich to be exhausted, that summons us to explore it and longs to be better known.

The mysterious seeks to remain hidden and evades explanation because, once brought into the light of day, it no longer exists.

There is never an end to understanding the mystery. But Latin and what it conceals is, for many people, something they have never even begun to understand. What is sacred is the object of our worship and the reality of the sacrament. By hiding these under the childish "mystery" of an unknown language you are cutting out the essential and confusing form with content.

Language and word are the instruments for the revelation of the mystery. You appreciate Latin because Latin adds to its concealment.

A sacrament is a sensible sign of a super-human reality which it suggests and signifies. As things are, principally because of Latin, the sign has become non-significant. The mystery has been sited in the means that should give people access to it. There is a grave risk that most people will never encounter it anywhere else.

Without words the sacramental rite is no longer a sign but a species of magic. A word whose sense is impenetrable is literally "hocus-pocus," not a word but a mere noise. The word means a relationship between two minds. It is the means by which the Spirit of God comes to my spirit. . . .

"But what a beautiful symbol it is of the unity of the Church! When one travels it is so moving to find that the Mass is the same in every part of the world."

There it is in a nutshell: so that strangers may feel everywhere at home, we have to feel strangers in our own country. And in any case, the unity of the Mass is not constituted by unity of language. Thank God! there are in the Catholic Church many recognized liturgical languages. The first Mass was said in Aramaic. This language soon gave way to Greek, so much more widely spoken. And when Greek itself became too scholarly a language, the liturgy was translated into Latin, the vulgar tongue, the language of the people—against whom it is today being maintained as a barrier.

"But what about those countries where there are several national languages? Wouldn't it be better for them to preserve Latin in order to avoid difficulties at linguistic frontiers?"

What a judgment of Solomon! A few may not understand. To avoid this, no one shall understand.

"But language evolves. In China the *Pater* and *Ave* were translated but after fifty years the language was so greatly changed that Christians could no longer understand them."

Is it really such a staggering feat to translate prayers every fifty years as an alternative to never understanding them at all? And you are ill-advised to take the example of the Chinese. It was Cardinal Constantini who said: "We have kept the Chinese at a distance from us, not by a wall of China but by a wall of Latin."

"Even if the epistle and gospel were proclaimed in French and with a loudspeaker, people still would not understand. The texts are too difficult."

What a light you throw on the state our religion has come to, when you say that. Preachers may perhaps in consequence be forced to comment on, to expound and show the relevance of the "sacred" texts of the Mass instead of using the Mass simply as a platform for the eloquence with which they speak of something else. The contemporary crisis of faith is, above all, for the faithful a crisis of invincible ignorance and for the clergy a crisis of sloth, of routine. Faith dies by a surfeit of fidelity to the letter and a famine of new thinking and fidelity to the spirit.

One day—and I hope it is not too far ahead—people will look back with astonishment at a time when priests and faithful were so sunk in apathy and formalism as to submit to the communal mouthing of the unintelligible.

The miracle of Pentecost, the miracle by which men first recognized the Catholic Church, was that each man heard the apostles speaking to him in his own tongue.

Some layfolk who attended an authentic, living, speaking Mass confided to me afterwards: "It was beautiful! To think that we might have died without ever knowing what a real Mass was like!"

How many people will die without ever having learned that?

The Offertory

The true Offertory at Mass is after the Consecration. Because it is not man but God who provides it. It is not man who gives himself. It is God who gives us what we can then give him. We do not go to Mass to offer ourselves but, fortunately, to offer the gift which the Son puts into our hands and which confers on us an unlimited power over the Father to give him joy and honour, to fill his heart with content in his children.

The joy of the Mass lies in receiving at one and the same time the grace of God and the means of expressing our gratitude. The Mass is a thanksgiving at which we celebrate the splendour of God's generosity, recount his benefits and rehearse his gifts, in order simultaneously to commemorate them, to give them back to him and with them to restore ourselves.

If the majority of Christians know nothing of the thanksgiving that is the Eucharist, that is because the Mass has never meant for them either a marvelling at the gift of God, or the best use to make of the gift, namely to give it back for the joy of him who gave it.

The Mass rite has become opaque and ambiguous. Something designed to instruct, now misleads. You can attend thousands of Masses and go deeper and deeper into confusion: ever more blindly identifying the celebration of the Word with the reading of the Gospel when in fact the true word, active, efficacious, penetrating, the true Gospel, the true Good News, is proclaimed at the Consecration: ever more hopelessly mistaking the Offertory for the bringing of human gifts, the Mass for an exchange between man who offers his bread and God who offers his Son, the great elevation for the little, the Mass for an initiation into the real Presence instead of a participation in the death and resurrection of Christ. The rite is no longer a highway into truth; it is like trampled ground, no longer giving any indication of route or direction but confusing them all.

The translation of the Mass into a living language will not be enough to give back signification to the sign, the sign itself will have to be restored and rescued from its own obscurity.

The Eucharistic Bread and Wine

For a long time I thought that, if I ever became Pope, I would change the matter of the sacraments and would take for the Eucharist the foodstuffs of the country: rice in China, seal meat in Greenland, bread fruit in Borneo, manioc in Africa.

For the Lord did not say: "My body is truly bread, my blood is truly wine." What he said was: "My flesh is truly food and my blood is truly drink." So could not any food or any drink become his flesh and his blood?

But nowadays I consider that this universal sameness of the sacred sign must be divinely willed.

We are tempted to take offence at the fact that the Church, the *Catholic* Church, should impose bread and wine as the matter of the sacrifice even in places where people eat no bread and never drink wine.

But could not that be the "sign" that our Christian duty is far broader than that of bringing them the Eucharist? Is not the duty of a Christian at the same time to procure bread for those who lack it, to share his bread with all those whom he invites to "communicate?"

We ought to bring them not only the sacrifice itself but also the matter of it for them to offer, once they have first been provided with it themselves. On the day when the Eucharist is celebrated through the length and breadth of the earth, what a richness of meaning, of symbolism, of unifying power will attach to this sole matter of the sacrifice, bread and wine. It will indeed serve fittingly for the Eucharist all over the world when it has been distributed all over the world by Catholic generosity.

As the Eucharist spreads over the world, it is the sign, it ought to be the sign, that the sharing of bread and wine is spreading too. The unity of the sacrifice should be preceded by the unification of men's hearts. "Go first and be reconciled with your brothers!" The Eucharist is the sign and source of sacrifice. It can be so fully only if it produces and spreads sacrifice in the same degree as it signifies sacrifice.

God's Failure

When the Lord looks down on one of our Sunday Masses, he must think he has completely failed with us. He whose purpose was to unite us one to the other ("Let them be one as we are one"), sees before him only people who may be willing to be united to him but under no circumstances to their neighbours. They come together in order to withdraw into solitude. They all come to do the same thing but to do it individually.

They are perfectly willing to come to Mass but on condition that they come when they like (late, of course); leave when they like (early—you've guessed!); sit wherever the fancy takes them (preferably near the door); adopt whatever posture they think fit (standing, sitting, kneeling, lying back); do something or do nothing as their whim suggests. That is all the communion (common-union), all the solidarity that they are capable of.

The slogan of a modern Mass is, "Every man for himself and God for all."

It must be a gloomy sight for God, all those Christians who so obviously don't get on together. How can they celebrate in honour of the Father when they present him with a family so apathetic and disunited? The son who is separated from his brethren is no longer a son and God does not know him. "Go first and be reconciled with your brother, then come and be reconciled with God." God has failed to teach us his love if he has not given us the power to share it with others.

Confession

How many priests have been crushed by the weight of Easter confessions, overwhelmed by the distress they cause?

They show so clearly what becomes of a sacrament when its use is brought down to a purely individualistic level.

The ordinary man, delivered over to his sole self, is all but incapable of self-examination, of repentance, of reformation and reparation such as is fitting. He needs the Church, that is to say, he needs the Holy Spirit acting within the community of his brethren. The people who come a year after their last confession and inform you that they have sometimes missed Sunday Mass ought not to be exhorted just for two minutes but for forty days. Lent should have restored to it the sense of penitence it once had, the sense of public confession within a set framework of instruction. Preparation for confession should be collective, as should repentance, penitence and reconciliation. An authentic celebration of the sacraments would restore to them their function of initiation, prayerful, expressive, efficacious and communal.

At the present day our sacraments are stifled, abbreviated, mutilated, reduced to private use in the same way as a low Mass has been reduced from a solemn High Mass.

Lent was originally reserved for public penitents. But when on Maundy Thursday the faithful saw the shining countenances of those who had done penance, they regretted that they had not all taken part in so fruitful a Lent. If on Ash Wednesday we receive a cross on our forehead, it is because we intend to pledge ourselves not to individual mortifications but to an organized and collective penance that will prepare us to receive in common the sacrament of penance.

Baptism

Baptism is the rite of Christian initiation, the rite from which we should have learnt to become Christians.

Formerly, its celebration was spread out over months and often over years; it instructed catechumens by prayerful ceremonies, readings, homilies, symbolic actions and fruitful rite.

But in our case, we were brought into the Church blind,

we became Christians without our knowledge and we start out on our catechumenate after having been baptized.

It will take us a long time to make up this handicap. Teaching a child the catechism in preparation for his first holy communion is a long way from being a replacement for the splendours of the baptismal liturgy. A syllogism is a poor exchange for a kiss.

We were lucky if we got the chance to be instructed by the baptismal liturgy at the christening of others. But the way these are performed is so impoverished; ceremonies that used to take forty days are crammed into twenty minutes. And it is all so individualistic; it is in solitude that we are incorporated into Christ. Whereas in fact a baptism is the Church welcoming and grafting on to itself a new member, we baptize in an empty church, in a remote corner, swiftly and almost furtively.

Why not a solemn celebration of baptism on Sunday afternoons instead of Vespers and Benediction, as there is a solemn celebration of the Eucharist on Sunday morning?

As the result of an excessively harsh and narrow theology of the "damnation" of children who die without baptism, we have given up collective baptism, we baptize birth by birth, as it were, and in any case many Christians of "good standing" would be upset to think of their children being baptized without distinction at the same time as other children.

And what a marvellous feast could be made too for the whole parish after the baptism of adults. The Church in which only babies are baptized is a Church living on its reserves.

It is such a pity, for example, that there is not a baptism at every Easter Vigil. An Easter Vigil without a baptism is like a Holy Week without the resurrection. The true resurrection of Christ, the true proof that Christ has risen, is baptism. This is because Christ is always living, always capable of coming to new life, always capable of raising to new life. A person baptized is a *"re-natus,"* one re-born. St Augustine said, "On that night [the night of the Easter Vigil] the pagans themselves did not sleep, tortured with restlessness and desire. In the town, at dawn, they gazed at the transformed countenances of new-made Christians. At the sight of them, many recognized Christ."

Pharisees

"You go to church," said St Paul to the Corinthians, "but it is not in order to become better, it makes you worse."

Some people would indeed be better if they were not Christians. They would be ashamed of the emptiness and self-absorption of their lives if they were not able to justify themselves by saying, "I go to Mass, I make my Easter duties." Unhappy man! Do you think you will achieve your salvation by swallowing a Host or turning up once a week for half-an-hour in church?

Ritual often lets us off truth. We go to communion, and that dispenses us from any need of sharing. We go to Mass and that excuses us from loving others. "I don't get on with my husband but I go to communion every day."

Pharisees are in fact people who would be better if they were not religious. Their good relations with God are made an excuse for their bad relations with other men. At the time of Christ they had come up with the idea of vowing their property to God so as to escape paying a pension for the food of aged parents. But of course property dedicated to God could not be used to pay a pension for the purchase of food! "I already have my work of piety. . . ." Having their accounts straight with regard to God gave their consciences a free hand for their accounts with other people.

Christ reversed all that. He told us: "Your accounts with God are the same as those with your neighbour. You are no closer to God than you are to your neighbour. The only proof that you love God is the fact that you love your neighbour."

And yet there are still Pharisees even within the Church of Christ.

The New Commandment

You can check the usefulness of your religious instruction by asking this simple question: "What is the new commandment? In what way is it new?"

Perhaps over half, well instructed, will give you the answer: "Love one another."

That is incorrect. That command existed already in the Old Testament. Christ is referring to it and the scribes give him their approval. The real newness of this evangelical precept consists in the fact that the second commandment is the same as the first. Fraternal charity is a theological virtue. He who loves God must love his brother. The man who asserts that he loves the God whom he does not see but does not love the brother whom he does see is a liar. The way we behave towards our neighbour is the revelation of our true attitude towards God.

And similarly, in Christianity, love of the brethren takes a sort of priority over love of the Father: "Go first and be reconciled with your brother." Because God is relatively easy to love. We invent him, we make up our own picture of him, we correct him, we set him at a distance or bring him close to us, we create him for our convenience, in our image and in our likeness. He isn't there to protest, he lets us do what we like to him. But our neighbour is different. If you love him, if you persevere in loving him, if you love all your neighbours, that is something miraculous, you absolutely must be doing something supernatural. You must be born of God, you are like God who also loves in this way.

In our creed, God becomes man. It is only there that he can be found with certainty. The last judgment will be a terrifying surprise; just and sinners alike will discover that God was their neighbour, that the first and the second commandments were *one and the same.*

Community

Why should Christians be community minded?

Because God is a community. He is not God prior to being three.

From all eternity he is God and from all eternity three, a community of persons totally transparent to each other, totally united with each other, such is their knowledge and love of each other. For God to be God there has to be more than one person. They had to be together in order to be themselves. They had to be several in order to be love. "*Non in unius singularitate personae. . . .*" How wonderful that you are not in solitude, how wonderful that you are several, how wonderful that you are love, we sing in the preface of the Blessed Trinity.

When man received existence as man, he was created in the image of God: he was created man and woman. That means he was created capable of loving, incapable of self-sufficiency, of finding fulfilment in himself, of a total turning in upon himself. He is made to give himself, to find his fulfilment in another, to set his joy in another. He is made to prefer himself in a being other than himself, made to know himself better and love himself better in the image that another being, in virtue of his own nature, reveals to him, a being that relieves him of the burden of his selfhood.

When we were baptized, we were incorporated into, grafted on to innumerable brothers. Cleaving to God bore for us the implication of beginning to cleave to others. God did not command us to love him alone but to love each other. He wanted us to become God for others, he wanted us to be like the God who loves those who do not deserve to be loved.

When we go to communion, our communion is with others; with the Host of our communion we take into ourselves all other men. Otherwise we shall not assimilate the Host, it will lie on our stomach and we must go and be reconciled with our brethren before we attempt to have communion with God at the altar.

When we go to confession we receive forgiveness only if we accept the duty of passing it on. We are forgiven only if we forgive. We are reconciled with God only if we are reconciled with our brethren. Our relationship with God and our relationship with others is one and the same. We are no nearer to God than we are to our neighbour.

And yet the religion of many Christians still boils down to this: "I say my prayers. I go to Mass. I make my private communion. I go to confession, if possible unbeknown to all others!" And you're lucky if they don't add: "And somebody else was sitting on my chair!"

Communicantes, united in a single communion. . . .

The Mystical Body

You are no closer to God than you are to your brother.

You have the same closeness to God as you have to your neighbour in the street, your neighbour at table, your neighbour at work or at Mass.

The Mass is the resurrection of Christ, becoming flesh once more as he incorporates us into himself. He has no body living here below other than that which is given to him by the ingathering of his members. The only way he can become alive among us is by bringing to birth within us a love that unites us with each other. When the members of Christ are united in love, Christ lives in their midst. But not when they remain in "separate bits."

The eucharistic bread is a bread that assimilates us into itself so that we may become all of us one sole and single bread, one sole and single body.

Being individualists, we exalt our miserable differences: I am poor, he is rich; I am important, he is not; I am intelligent, he is stupid. And we forget the marvellous family bond in which we are alike: he is of Christ, and so am I.

Who among us would accept to be his neighbour?

We are difficult to please, quickly put off, wilfully fastidious. But for his part, Christ is willing to become anyone at all. He gives himself to anyone at all. Anybody can bear him away within him in his own life.

If you become Christ, are you not consenting to become anyone at all?

Your refusal of communion with others is an effect of your undervaluing your baptism. Can you remember where you were baptized? And on what day it was? You do remember your birth on this earth—and to the earth you will return. But your birth in Christ, do you remember it, value it, give thanks for it? Have you ever given thanks for being baptized?

By baptism you became a member of Christ. You were incorporated into him. What is most alive in you, most real in you, what is alone alive in you, is Christ. The only thing in you which will in all eternity be alive is that which, in you, has been incorporated into Christ.

That is what the priest means when he says to you at Communion: "*Corpus Domini. . .*" "May the body of Christ keep your soul living unto eternal life." You can cleave to God only by entering into a body. What saves your soul is to become one body with others.

At Mass you come to reaffirm your baptism, perfect your incorporation, render the body of Christ more alive.

The Lamb of God takes away the sins of the world (there is only one sin: refusal to love) precisely by restoring our capacity to love one another.

When shall we understand that it is vain for us to go to Mass if, when we leave it, we love our neighbour no better? Do you think that Christ could have become alive in you without your loving your brethren?

Adam and Judas

All they lacked was faith. They couldn't give God the benefit of the doubt, couldn't prefer his plan to their plans, his will to theirs. "For even as the heavens are raised above the earth, so are his ways above our ways and his thoughts above our thoughts."

They wanted to touch, embrace, taste their reward and their kingdom, instead of waiting to receive it from the hand of God, waiting with an unshakeable faith.

Even in paradise, faith was already needed! Adam was lord and king of the world, but God demanded of him that he should trust him in the matter of a fruit, of a tree, of a single "secret" of the Lord. And Adam could not do it. He wanted to take into his own hands the hidden providence of the Lord. He wanted to handle, taste, savour, profane the mystery. He wanted to get it into his power, subdue it to his will, have it under his control. And he lost everything.

Judas had his own private ideas about the redemption. It was to begin with him and his friends. It was to be done for their benefit and they were going to rise far because of it. When Christ declared his opposition, Judas decided that, one way or another, the profit he expected was not going to escape him.

What his hand closed on was money, thanks to his refusal to believe in that kingdom which cannot be localized. All he put into his pocket was thirty pieces of silver because he could not bring himself to make an act of trust in God.

Like Adam, like us, he preferred to die rather than believe.

Exposition of the Blessed Sacrament

Devotion to the sacramental body of Christ often goes hand in hand with an astonishing indifference to his real body. Yet the Host before which we bow down is, before all else, a food. If nobody eats it, it loses all its meaning. When the Blessed Sacrament is raised before the people it would be a good idea to suggest they should think of the man who will make his communion with the Host which they are venerating. That would certainly be a bit of a shock for them, would spoil their appetite. They are willing enough to love God, to swallow God, but not their neighbour. That is asking a bit too much. That really would give them indigestion.

And yet, swallowing a Host to make sure of one's salvation would really be too easy, were it not that this communion signifies that you accept to take into yourself all other men, to unite yourself to all other men, were it not that it is the sign and the source of that union of Christians among themselves which is the only authentic proof of their union with God.

The Eucharist is a sacrament, but where there is no union with our brethren, it may well be asked what has become of the sacrifice. The man who tries to unite himself to the God whom he does not see but who refuses or neglects to unite himself to his brethren whom he does see, is a liar.

You must have heard people speak with horror of those who steal the sacramental species in order to defile and mutilate them. But it disturbs us infinitely less to be in the presence of those who, by their hatred, their prejudices, their egoism or simply their indifference, tear at the true body of Christ.

Which is graver, to violate the means or the end, the food or the person, the bread or the Body?

At the Last Judgment we shall not be asked whether we adored Christ in the Eucharist, but whether we loved our brethren in the way that adoration should have taught us to.

Advent

Chesterton, in *Manalive*, has the idea of a husband who, in order to keep the experience of their love from ever growing cold, every year wins his wife afresh under a new disguise and in different circumstances.

The press reports a disturbing increase in the rate of abduction in England. An enquiry is opened. The public get emotionally involved. A suspect is arrested and, in the course of the investigation, this further scandalous detail is discovered, that it is invariably the same man who carries off all these young women.

The trial proceeds . . . until the moment when it is discovered that every case without exception involves . . . the same woman.

God, like the boldest of lovers, gives us the most improbable rendezvous: a poor man, a cross, a husband, our parish priest, a bit of bread, a difficult and unhappy old man, a peevish child. Scarcely have we begun to recognize him, to let him in under one form, than he reappears under another.

And we, like obsessed and panic-stricken old maids, are shocked and scandalized anew and find each new development all but impossible to adjust to. In vain God tries to prepare the way by overwhelming us with tenderness. Every time we are caught unprepared and he, coming unexpectedly, finds our heart so poverty-stricken, so empty of the love with which he should be received.

No! This mustn't, this won't happen always! One day we shall join in the game, we shall play it with God, with the same joy and the same ironic tenderness with which he played with us. And when the next trial or indeed the same one (the one we had been dreading since yesterday or perhaps all our lives) comes towards us with that alien and forbidding countenance, we shall lovingly lift off his mask to smile at our Beloved. "Blessed is that man," said Jesus, "who is not scandalized by the way in which I come to him."

Christmas

I often think that, at Christmas, our Lord's sudden arrival on the scene would be enough to spoil all our celebrations. If Jesus invited himself into our hearts (even without his family), whether under the appearance of a displaced person, one of those old men left behind in refugee camps whom nobody wants because they are old, foreigners and useless, or in the form of a juvenile delinquent, on three days' holiday, or in the guise of an aged aunt (with no money to leave) or an old uncle (not coming from America), sick and coming under our roof only to die, well, that would be the end of our celebrations, Christmas would be spoilt. What discomfort he would cause, what hard feelings, what havoc, what violent reactions! Your husband would protest, or your wife would complain, your maid would give notice, your children would declare that they would rather spend Christmas somewhere else—and you would be all alone, with nobody to give you their approval.

Every time our Lord has ever invaded a person's life, he has shaken it from top to bottom. Think for a moment: Zacchaeus, after the Lord had passed by, was left without a penny! (This does occasionally happen at Christmas to the father of a family, but not often for religious motives.) But Zacchaeus was overflowing with joy and liberty of heart, and as he gave out his gold to the poor, he felt an immeasurably greater satisfaction than in the amassing of it.

Think of Mary. She can never have felt poorer, more destitute, more deprived, more abandoned than when the Lord was born. He chose the worst possible moment and the most awkward place. She was a refugee, a "displaced person," and nobody wanted to take her under their roof. But it was then that she knew joy, and we can be sure that never in all the world was there a greater one.

People look back with longing towards the first Christmas. They are sad to think they did not live at the time when Christ could be touched and seen and embraced.

But they forget that this was also the time when he was recognized, loved, revered by practically nobody. Above all they forget that that time has not yet come to an end, that the light is still shining in darkness, that the Word has been made flesh and dwells among us, that he is ever among his own but his own neither recognize nor receive him.

To complain of the fact that we did not live in that time is the best possible proof that we are actually living in that time. Because at that time too people had their complaints. At that time too the presence of God among his own contradicted expectations, demanded renunciation, caused pain. It called men to sacrifice, to generosity and to faith. And Jesus said, for us as much as for his contemporaries: "Blessed is that man who is not scandalized by the way in which I come to him."

The Passion this Year

This is the beginning of Lent, the Passion is beginning again. Jesus is going to be crucified once more, Jesus is going to suffer all over again, Jesus is suffering again among us. What part have you chosen to play in the action?

The Gospel is not a legend, it is not even a piece of past history. It is a prophecy. It foretells to us what is and always will be happening in the world. It is a living revelation, unceasingly relevant, that discloses to us the true meaning of what is happening under our very eyes. The Gospel discloses to us the life of God among men. God lives unceasingly among men. Jesus is with us all days even to the consummation of the age; Jesus is our contemporary and the Gospel speaks to us of what is happening this very day between him and us, how Jesus is treating us and how we are treating him. You are described in the Gospel, you are there foreseen and named—you have only to open the book to recognize yourself in its pages.

The Passion is beginning; it involves today the same rôles and the same actors as always.

Well, first of all there are the millions and millions of the indifferent, the cowards, those who give their tacit consent, who wash their hands of the business, who make no move so long as it is only someone else who is being hit, those who will venture no opinion on those disputed questions, who let things take their course—people without whom these things could never be. The malice of a few can build on sure foundations in the cowardice of all.

How many injustices, how many terrible scenes have we looked on with this same criminal indifference?

Then there are the thousands of fugitives, people who

at awkward moments, like St Peter, "no longer know that man." Oh! they've heard him preaching, they've been moved, it made them feel so good afterwards; they joined in the demonstrations, they were to be seen in all the processions, they were enthusiastic about the miracles, in fact they would have gone a long way to see a miracle, they would have gone to Lourdes or Fatima! But now that things are going badly, when it has all turned sour, when there's blood and a Cross, now that there are no more miracles but we are expected to be miracles of loyalty, faith and love, they want nothing more to do with him, they no longer know the man, they act as if they had never heard of him.

There are a few thousand executioners too; they are never lacking, they are always the same: the brute with his whip, the scientist with his injections, the administrator with his forms, the onlooker with his curiosity.

And there is the same sorrowful victim, infinitely patient and loving, gazing at us with a look that speaks a question, a look full of tenderness, expectation and reproach. There are more victims than ever before, more just men suffering, more innocents persecuted: twelve million orphaned or disabled by war, hundreds of thousands of displaced persons, old people without a use they can be put to, offered to all takers on every square of Europe and there are no takers; 30,000 Greek children, a true massacre of the innocents, torn away from their fathers and mothers and exiled in a fratricidal war. Millions and millions of convicts, still living as it seems in Russian concentration camps. The millions of refugees and the millions of the shelterless in Korea and Vietnam—but why should we go so far away? Is there nobody right beside you, are there no people around you, suffering, weeping, enduring cold or hunger or sickness, bowed down under the weight of a bereavement, of loneliness, of a sickness or even simply of their own difficult character? They are there and they are waiting for you. Who will be Veronica, who will be Simon of Cyrene? Come on, the parts are being given out, there isn't much time. Everyone must take what suits him. No one can evade choosing. Who will be John? Who will be Peter? Who will be Judas?

How marvellously lucky we are! Jesus is here, he is living among us, he is suffering once again. He is beginning to suffer. And we have been warned, we know what is going on, we have been told all about it, we have been given the key of this terrible tragedy, the real name of the actor has been whispered to us, the real meaning of the drama. Come on, there is nothing left for us to do but to join in, to intervene. What a joy it is that we can choose our own rôle, we can be for him whatever we choose to be, we can bring it about that, in the endless crowd of the indifferent and the hostile, there should be a few servants watching, a few hearts waiting, a few faces loving, a few gestures of reverence, limitless compassion, weeping adoration. Come on, that's the way things are, we know it perfectly well, it isn't even faith that we lack, alas, it is only courage.

Lent

It would be much better to speak of the "vivifications" of Lent rather than recommending mortifications.

Our Christians are a good deal too "mortified." They are so deadened by it all that any supplementary mortifications would be an unbearable burden. A man has to be well and truly alive to endure being hacked about.

Authentic Lenten resolutions concern such things as praying for an extra quarter of an hour a day, going to confession more frequently, going to Mass and to communion.

God, once he has become alive in us, will then allow us to do without the rest.

Normally the rest allows us to do without God.

What I mean to say is that our whole way of life is organized in such a way as to let us do without God. In the same way as Trappists and Carmelites work out their way of life to make it humanly impossible to bear it without endlessly having recourse to God, we have multiplied distractions, pleasures and sins in such a way as to make our life endurable to us without him.

Only the divine presence, only God, becoming once more alive for us, can give us the power to do without everything which normally dispenses us from paying him attention.

The Way of the Cross

The Passion, the redemption—I think many of us began to understand and accept what it means only after the revelation of the war and the concentration camps.

Before the war, before the fearful revelation that the same passion for evil dwelt in the hearts of our contemporaries, the scene of the mocking, Jesus at the pillar, Jesus crowned with thorns, Jesus stripped of his clothes, Jesus crucified, all these things seemed to us so many scenes from a different age, crudely drawn pictures full of violence, prints of a time before our own. But ever since we saw with our own eyes, ever since our friends told us their stories, ever since what our parents endured, the Gospel has, for many of us, suddenly come to life.

People have once again sensed the stranger at work, the

prince of darkness roaming round about us, the evil one, the tempter with his despair. Around us we felt so much evil and within us so much weakness and helplessness.

We thought of our brothers and friends who had been taken away; our hearts were shaken with pity and anger. But it was a joy as well to think that Jesus had lived through, had endured all that; how proud we felt of God, and what immense consolation we felt as we thought that his love had gone with them, had gone before them even to such a destination. At one time or another, they must have thought of this, they must have met him, they must have realized where they were. At one or another of the stations of their private way of the cross, they must have realized that Love had suddenly joined them, had sought them out.

When they in their turn were stripped of their garments, perhaps that was the moment when, for the first time, they understood why Jesus had chosen to let himself be stripped of his garments; they exchanged a glance with him, they understood and recognized each other.

When they were beaten up and humiliated, perhaps for a moment the thought came to them of him whom they had become; they understood why Jesus had been willing to be mocked and scourged; they understood what a love it was, humble, silent, faithful, that had been waiting for them down the ages.

When, on death marches, they collapsed with exhaustion, they realized that their falls were the continuation of Another's and that this was their entry into the communion of a marvellous brotherhood.

Transcending all time and space, someone had been thinking of them, someone had followed them, someone had undergone all things so as to be there by their side, so that, even when the whole world had abandoned them and our love could no longer protect or help them, there should remain to them one single friend, a comrade in chains, a comrade at the cross, and there should come to meet them the purest, noblest, most tender and consoling image of what they had become.

Christ became God on Calvary

Did Christ know that he was God?

When asked such a question, we must above all avoid any sort of "notional" response (cf. the catechism: "God is a pure spirit, infinite in perfection and the source of all good").

Christ knew that he was the Son. For Christ, to be God means to be the Son, but so entirely, so fully, that everything which is the Father's, the Son receives and everything that the Father does, the Son learns to do.

He grew in age and in wisdom before God and before men. He became more and more filial.

That is why it is possible to say that Jesus became God on Calvary. "Son though he was, the experience of suffering was needed for him to learn the meaning of obedience."

However astonishing it may sound, to be God means to obey. It means an absolute setting of one's heart on another, a total obedience, a perfect consent, a love than which there can be no greater: to give one's life for the beloved. God is pure availability for another. He is pure gift—it is like what a bird would be if it were pure flight. A man is reserved and turned in on himself. Our personal antonomy is never more than the residue of a certain incapacity for self-giving.

When, in the Gospel, Christ said: "Father, all that is yours is mine," and added, "all that is mine is yours," did you understand that this was not a motion of gratitude, a gesture of courtesy? He is simply expressing an identity.

What belongs to God is to love, to give. If Christ has received this in full measure, then he must show it by giving in his turn. His love is the revelation of the love with which he has been loved.

We ought not to say: Christ could have redeemed us by a single drop of his blood.

We should say: All the sufferings of Christ are the revelation of that detachment which is needed to love truly.

The obstacle to holiness is not simply the fact of being a sinner, it is the fact of being human. Christ, who, like Mary, had committed no sin, had to learn the painful renunciation of his personal will. In God, love is a joyful gift; in man, it is a painful renunciation. God is a drive towards another, an ecstasy, a subsisting relationship. Man is a separate and autonomous being, never-endingly tempted to self-sufficiency within his own personal subsistence. In order to become totally God, Christ had totally to renounce himself.

Only one's Joy must be crucified

The Gospel begins in an immense burst of joy: the two annunciations, the promises, the miracles, the calling of the apostles, the friendship, the wonder, the presence, the tenderness of God dwelling among us.

The lesson we had first to learn, the message that had most urgently to be conveyed, was that God was infinitely more loving, more desirable, more dazzling than we had ever imagined. Our great, our principal, our most urgent duty was to exult, to give thanks, to be astounded, to be first overwhelmed and then exalted, to weep and to laugh, to kiss his hands and his feet, to halt only to grasp more perfectly what was happening and then to start again.

Ah! there was no value in the sacrifices we performed, in the agony, in the stupor, in the error of our belief that we were alone and in the error of our sometimes judging that we were better than the God to whom those sacrifices were made! It is good to offer sacrifice but we did it badly, we were not worthy of the good we were performing. This good was for us a source of evil.

Jesus came to spread joy. All who opened themselves to him, all who let themselves be won over to his love, were filled by him with his joy, it was his will that they should overflow with joy.

Ah! Let us not speak of sacrifice, of passion, of the cross. We first of all have to learn, we first of all have to realize who Jesus is, to be overwhelmed by his loving-kindness, his love, the joy of his tenderness, and then, but only then, everything else follows. Slowly love becomes conscious of itself, of its own strength, of the demands of its own nature. It feels itself growing and ripening towards more manly tasks, towards ever bolder forms of love. . . . It knows ever more clearly what it is and what it loves. It desires with ever more purity to express this. It concentrates more and more on essentials—less talking, more doing. Then, it sees, it begins to understand what might be an adequate way of bearing witness to such a joy. It feels itself flooded at last with the peace that belongs to a love that can go no further, the peace of knowing one has been found worthy to experience and to practise the highest form of love. And so love sets its joy upon the cross!

Together with its joy, love mounts upon the cross, in order to express and reaffirm it, so that none may doubt it, to know at last the relief of having uttered it so perfectly, of having expressed it so completely, with its tears, its cries, its prayers and its incomparable peace.

Jesus mounted the cross with his joy: "so that the world may know that I love my Father and that I obey the command which my Father has given me. . . ." He showed what a son can do in his devotion for his father.

He crucified only his joy.

Will you rise from the dead?

Who wants unending life? Who finds life good enough to desire it without end? Is there anything in your life that you would like to make eternal?

We assert our belief "in the resurrection of the body and in life everlasting"—but with such a total lack of interest that it is exactly as if we didn't believe in it at all: we never give it a moment's thought!

We moderns, instead of casting doubt on our faith in the resurrection, should begin by asking ourselves questions about our desire to rise from the dead.

Among all the people you meet, busy, blasé, restless, do you know any who look as if they want all that much to go on for ever?

Even those who lead a life of "pleasure," can you see them condemned to forced pleasure in perpetuity? They would far prefer forced labour!

Eternal life? Who wants it?

How can we preach the resurrection to people who no longer value life?

I think that faith in the resurrection can arise only from a great and authentic love. Love conceives such faith, and that faith reveals the love. Lovers spontaneously promise to love each other for ever, and that is the only sign by which a true love is recognized.

Our faith in and our hope of the resurrection, both for ourselves and for others, depends a great deal on our capacity for loving. What do we value enough to eternalize, and to eternalize ourselves with it? What I mean is this: does there exist one being, one achievement, one state of soul that you value sufficiently highly to desire it to be part of your eternity? And does there exist a being that you love enough to make you want to be eternal because of it?

Our capacity for redemption and resurrection, both on our own behalf and that of others, is in direct proportion to our power of loving.

It cannot really be said we shall have a lot to eternalize!

Blessed is that man who has discovered in his life even a single moment that he would like to make eternal! Blessed is that man who does that which is so much more than simply believing in the resurrection: who lives a life capable of being resurrected.

Witnesses of the Resurrection

The best proof that Christ has risen is that he is still alive. And for the immense majority of our contemporaries, the only way of seeing him alive is for us Christians to love one another.

There is only one proof that Christ is still alive: the fact that love is still living here on earth, *his* love, that goes to the point of giving its life for those he loves.

Christ has no visible body apart from Christians, and no other love to show mankind but theirs. It is for us to bear witness to the resurrection of Christ.

Shame on that religion whose proofs are all in the past! The reason why, at the present moment, the masses fall away into apostasy while an élite is converted, is this: it is possible nowadays to prove the resurrection of Christ by reading, study and research of a kind limited to intellectuals, but the masses, the poor, the humble, will never be convinced by all that; they have to be content with seeing and watching, seeing us and watching us, us Christians—and they are never going to opt for the sacrifices demanded by a conversion whose only result is the privilege of looking like us!

Christians of every epoch have the duty of working out the form Christ's incarnation should take in their milieu, the mode of his presence to their contemporaries. Every disciple of Christ is the father and mother of the Lord (Mark 3.35). The duty of each Christian is to bring the Lord into the world, giving him the chance of coming to life again by lending him his hands so that there may be gestures of love, his lips so that he may pronounce words of love, his heart and conscience so that love may still shine out over the world.

"There where two or three are gathered together in my name—that is to say, are united in, love each other with my love—I am in the midst of them," says the Lord. The charity of the Church, an authentic liturgical life, Christian marriage, truly fervent religious communities, apostolic priests and laity, these are the pledges and the proofs of Christ's resurrection.

Our world is full of despair and doubt, groping for the wounds of the risen Christ; may it find in us proofs of his living presence beyond all doubting: open heart, open hands, a welcome full of love and compassion, and hear the gentle reproach: "Because you have seen, Thomas, you have believed!"

The glory and the manifestation of the power of the risen Christ is to have raised up to himself a body!

"If you loved me, you would rejoice that I go to the Father"

Offer God the sacrifice of being happy.

The great virtue we should exercise during Paschaltide is joy.

At every moment the prayer of the Church at Mass or in the Office is interrupted by cries of joy, by endless Alleluias. And Jesus tells us that this joy is what will distinguish us from "the world": "Yet a little while," he said on the eve of his Passion, "and the world will see me no longer; but you, you will see me, I shall see you again and your heart will rejoice and no one will take your joy from you."

Now the odd thing is that we are not in tune with this joy. We are more ready to sorrow with Christ than to rejoice with him; we find it easier to share his sufferings than his joy.

The greatest sacrifice and most searching renunciation that we must offer to God is to be happy.

Yes, in this age of pessimism, of international tension, of distress and doubt, one must lay heavy stress on this duty of being happy.

We are like St Thomas. You know that all the information we get on him from the gospels is two traits of character that, superficially, seem to contradict each other. When Jesus was on his way to raise Lazarus from the dead, the disciples in terror said to him: "Master, the Jews were wanting to stone you, and are you going back there?" Jesus answered that they must have confidence and that no evil can touch them so long as they walk in his company. And Thomas says to the other apostles: "Let us go and die with him!" This was not an utterance of faith nor of real generosity, it was the sign of a bitter and deep seated pessimism like that which later on will prompt him so vigorously to reject the proclamation of the resurrection.

Well, we are like him, pessimists, courageous perhaps in the sense that we don't refuse suffering but unwilling at any price to believe in happiness. During Lent, for example, perhaps we mortified ourselves, or at any rate thought of doing so; we went to the Lenten services, and who hasn't felt that Good Friday is a day different from all other days?

But once Easter has come, once the Resurrection has happened, our religious life takes a holiday, we have come to the end, as we think, of the liturgical year, with a sense of relief, but also of finality that goes with Holy Saturday, we no longer see what part is left for us to play.

And yet there is something quite specially self-centred and hard-hearted in the refusal to take part in the joy of a friend, in accepting only his sufferings, in abandoning him at the very moment when we could give him the greatest of all joys: that of letting him do good for us.

But the true explanation of this attitude is at a deeper level. We are more ready to afflict and mortify ourselves with our Lord than to rejoice in his resurrection, because what we are looking for in suffering is ourselves, what we so easily find is ourselves: our naturally pessimistic turn of mind is in tune with those tragic events, and we always have good reasons for being sad on our own account, which allow us to feel sorry for ourselves while appearing to feel sorry for him.

But to share in the joy of another, that is the occasion and the sign of a genuine devotion and disinterestedness, because it is a joy in which there is nothing of us, a joy in which we find so little of ourselves.

After Lent, the greatest mortification of all is still to come, the greatest renunciation of all still has to be made, the one prepared by all the others and the touchstone of their authenticity: We must offer God the sacrifice of being happy. We must give God the joy and reward of seeing us happy, of telling him that after all he has done and suffered on our behalf, there really is nothing else we can live on save the joy of his love; we are bound up with him, united to him, we live by him, so that when we look into the depths of ourselves, we find that nothing in us is more living than his joy.

"It is good for you that I go away"

We are privileged people, with many advantages denied to Christ's contemporaries. He asserts this. We know it. Do we believe it?

The history of Christ's birth, of his life, of his apparent defeat by reason of man's lack of faith, was lived through long ago. We have meditated on it, mourned it, told others about it.

Do we realize that we are living it?

God has come back for us. The Holy Spirit who re-utters for us all that Jesus has done, is the author of the sacraments which re-present all that Jesus underwent.

The sacraments are the place where, whenever we so choose, we can render ourselves present afresh at the birth, the death and the resurrection of Christ.

The Christ event is of infinitely greater richness, power and splendour in the sacraments than in the facts of Jesus' human history.

If we took part with faith in the celebration of the sacraments, we would have a share in the life of the Lord, we should have a communion with his existence, far beyond anything that would have been ours, had we every day stood in the midst of the crowd of those that listened to him.

Every time we celebrate the Eucharist with authenticity, we do it very much better than the disciples at the Last Supper when Jesus said to Peter: "What I am doing now, you do not know. But afterwards you will understand."

St John wrote the loveliest of all the gospels because he wrote the last. The Holy Spirit had had time to repeat to him all that Jesus had said. St John had been present too at many baptisms, at many Eucharists.

The fact that St John tells us so much and with such splendour is not in virtue of his having been a witness of special attentiveness the first time, it is because he had the chance to be a witness at an ever increasing depth on an infinite number of occasions, it is because his was the most faithful and reverent attention to that presence of the Lord which is perpetuated, renewed, continued for ever in the sacraments.

Every time the apostles celebrated the Eucharist together, they were celebrating the Lord's presence among them, a presence guaranteed and promised for ever. He was there in the midst of them, better known, better loved, more active than before. They knew now who he was. Their awareness of their own power gave them an extraordinary pride and assurance. They were sure of their power to renew the presence of the Lord among them in proportion to their own needs, faith and love.

The Ascension

(Mark 16.14-20)

The only way of making the Ascension into a feast day is to grasp the distinction between a disappearance and a departure. A departure causes an absence. A disappearance is the inauguration of a hidden presence.

By his Ascension, Christ becomes invisible; he enters into his share of the omnipotence of the Father; he is fully glorified in his humanity, and, in virtue of that, is more than ever related with each one of us.

If the Ascension had been Christ's departure, we would have been right to mourn and regret it. Fortunately it is nothing of the kind. Christ remains with us all days, even to the consummation of the age, but he acquires at his Ascension that boundless extension of his power that enables him to fill all things with his presence. St Paul says: "He went up to heaven in order to fill all things with his presence" (Eph. 4.10).

We must neither bury Christ on earth nor bury him in heaven! His Ascension marks an increase of power and of effectiveness, an intensification of his presence, of which the Eucharist bears witness. It is not simply an ascension through space, which could only result in a withdrawal from us: "Do not stay here gazing up to heaven, but work on to extend his kingdom and his presence by perfecting his work here below," say the angels to the apostles.

Christ remains the most active personality in the history of the world.

St Mark expresses this idea in a striking way in his account of the Ascension: "Jesus was raised to heaven where he is seated on the right hand of God."

There it is, we think, we've lost him. He has left us. He sits for ever on his throne above while we trudge on here below.

But St Mark goes on: "The apostles went off and preached everywhere. The Lord worked with them and supported their preaching by the miracles which accompanied it."

What joy this is! He is here, on earth, with us, and never again will he leave us because his presence, now made spiritual, has achieved an intensity and an extension of which his physical presence would always have been incapable.

It was to our advantage that he should depart in a visible manner, so that we should find him everlastingly and everywhere present in an invisible manner.

The Feast of the Sacred Heart

To become the person whom God loves in us

HE LOVED US FIRST . . .

The Greeks thought that it was man who, in pursuit of his own perfection, sought God.

God, motionless and self-sufficient, remained the indifferent focus of all our strivings.

The Pharisees admitted that God loves men, but they had canalized, regulated, rationalized this love.

God loved the just, so they thought, in proportion to their justice and hated sinners to the full measure of their sins.

That which Jesus revealed, a scandal for the Jews and

a folly for the Gentiles, was that God's love for us is gratuitous, that he seeks out the lost, lives familiarly and even "eats with sinners," loves the sinner in spite of his sin, and the just man also, but not because of his justice, but rather without cause, madly, gratuitously, like all true lovers. Our mothers and fathers love us, not by reason of our qualities and virtues, but out of the goodness of their own hearts, so warm, so strong, so faithful that they are confident of arousing one day, within us too, a love like theirs.

Two categories of people are thus for ever excluded from salvation: the hypocrites who fear true love and are satisfied with conventions, and the proud.

We are not hypocrites: we do sincerely seek after God. But we are all proud.

I don't mean that we are necessarily among those who demand of God that he love them for their justice and show them sinners punished and condemned for their sins. . . .

But we all come into the category of the proud who refuse to be loved *before* they deserve it.

We make tremendous efforts to become more worthy or less unworthy of being loved by God, before we admit, before we believe that he does actually love us. We site God in *our future*, as an ideal to be attained, as the crowning of our moral conquests.

God is not merited: he gives himself. God is not conquered: he offers himself. God is not above us but below us; he is waiting for us at the level at which he found Zacchaeus, at which he converted Mary Magdalene, and we shall never find him unless we let ourselves go in his arms. God is not out ahead of us: he is behind us.

What we want is to win God, whereas it is already so difficult to *accept* him as he gives himself to us. Like the Jews, we wait for him to come—O glorious reward!—on the clouds of heaven, revealing his favour at long last for all those who fought in solitude and obscurity for his greater glory.

And yet he has always been there, in the thick of the battle, unrecognized, abandoned, despised, eaten in bread, drunk in wine, mocked in the most insignificant of men, shoulder to shoulder with us, so close that our eyes always look beyond him.

"You must not try to snatch our Lord's love before you have known it."

"He loves us without our being worthy of it, let us love him without being worthy of it."

"He loved us first."

From all eternity God loves us in that part of ourselves in which the tide of his presence has risen slowly and irresistibly, in spite of our dams and defences.

God finds his joy and his delight in one whole part of ourselves on which he has worked so patiently, which he fosters and cherishes like a Father. From all eternity God loves us, from long before our least thought of him, long before we ever knew him.

What really interests us is our future; what we lack and what we intend to get, that narrow beach in front of us on whose sand we write our will.

But our true future is behind us: our true future is to achieve a total likeness to the person that from all eternity God loves in us.

Nothing so humbles, nothing so strips us as this certitude that we have already been broken into, that we have been forestalled by a love so strong and faithful that ours in comparison must appear desperately unstable and mean.

Jesus, what did you do to make your way into this heart so jealous of its independence, this heart so proudly sensitive that another's mere intent to love can repel it, this lazy, greedy heart that grows weary the moment after it began to love, this weak heart which beats no more than just enough to live, and which, my Master, you chose should learn to beat for love?

OTHER IMAGE BOOKS

A 74-1

OTHER IMAGE BOOKS

A WOMAN CLOTHED WITH THE SUN – Edited by John J. Delaney (D118) – $1.45

INTERIOR CASTLE – St. Teresa of Avila (Translated by E. Allison Peers) – (D120) – $1.45

THE GREATEST STORY EVER TOLD – Fulton Oursler (D121) – $1.45

LIVING FLAME OF LOVE – St. John of the Cross (Translated by E. Allison Peers) – (D129) – $1.45

A HISTORY OF PHILOSOPHY: VOLUME 1 – GREECE AND ROME (2 Parts) – Frederick Copleston, S.J. (D134a, D134b) – $1.75 ea.

A HISTORY OF PHILOSOPHY: VOLUME 2 – MEDIAEVAL PHILOSOPHY (2 Parts) – Frederick Copleston, S.J. Part I – Augustine to Bonaventure. Part II – Albert the Great to Duns Scotus (D135a, D135b) – $1.75 ea.

A HISTORY OF PHILOSOPHY: VOLUME 3 – LATE MEDIAEVAL AND RENAISSANCE PHILOSOPHY (2 Parts) – Frederick Copleston, S.J. Part I – Ockham to the Speculative Mystics. Part II – The Revival of Platonism to Suárez (D136a, D136b) – $1.45 ea.

A HISTORY OF PHILOSOPHY: VOLUME 4 – MODERN PHILOSOPHY: Descartes to Leibniz – Frederick Copleston, S.J. (D137) – $1.75

A HISTORY OF PHILOSOPHY: VOLUME 5 – MODERN PHILOSOPHY: The British Philosophers, Hobbes to Hume (2 Parts) – Frederick Copleston, S.J. Part I – Hobbes to Paley (D138a) – $1.45. Part II – Berkeley to Hume (D138b) – $1.75

A HISTORY OF PHILOSOPHY: VOLUME 6 – MODERN PHILOSOPHY (2 Parts) – Frederick Copleston, S.J. Part I – The French Enlightenment to Kant (D139a) – $1.45; (D139b) – $1.75

A HISTORY OF PHILOSOPHY: VOLUME 7 – MODERN PHILOSOPHY (2 Parts) – Frederick Copleston, S.J. Part I – Fichte to Hegel. Part II – Schopenhauer to Nietzsche (D140a, D140b) – $1.75 ea.

A HISTORY OF PHILOSOPHY: VOLUME 8 – MODERN PHILOSOPHY: Bentham to Russell (2 Parts) – Frederick Copleston, S.J. Part I – British Empiricism and the Idealist Movement in Great Britain. Part II – Idealism in America, the Pragmatist Movement, the Revolt against Idealism (D141a, D141b) – $1.45 ea.

A DOCTOR AT CALVARY – Pierre Barbet, M.D. A moving account of the Passion of our Lord (D155) – 95¢

These prices subject to change without notice

OTHER IMAGE BOOKS

OTHER IMAGE BOOKS

GUIDE TO CONTENTMENT – Fulton J. Sheen (D282) – $1.45
THE PSALMS OF THE JERUSALEM BIBLE – Alexander Jones, General Editor (D283) – $1.45
THE PEOPLE ARE THE CHURCH – Eugene C. Kennedy (D284) – $1.25
CONTEMPLATIVE PRAYER – Thomas Merton (D285) – 95¢
THE CHALLENGES OF LIFE – Ignace Lepp (D286) – $1.25
THE ROMAN CATHOLIC CHURCH – John L. McKenzie (D287) – $1.75
LIFE FOR A WANDERER – Andrew M. Greeley (D288) – $1.25
BEING TOGETHER: OUR RELATIONSHIPS WITH OTHER PEOPLE – Marc Oraison (D289) – $1.25
MARRIAGE IS FOR GROWNUPS – Joseph and Lois Bird (D291) – $1.45
THE FRIENDSHIP GAME – Andrew M. Greeley (D292) – $1.25
HOW TO BE REALLY WITH IT – Bernard Basset, S.J. (D293) – $1.25
THE ABORTION DECISION – Revised Edition – David Granfield (D294) – $1.45
MEETING GOD IN MAN – Ladislaus Boros, S.J. (D295) – $1.25
AUTHORITY IN THE CHURCH – John L. McKenzie (D296) – $1.25
A TIME FOR LOVE – Eugene C. Kennedy (D297) – $1.25
CHRIST IS ALIVE! – Michel Quoist (D298) – $1.25
THE MAN IN THE SYCAMORE TREE: The Good Times and Hard Life of Thomas Merton – Edward Rice (D299) – $1.95
THE NEW TESTAMENT OF THE NEW AMERICAN BIBLE (D300) – $1.75
INTRODUCTION TO THE DEVOUT LIFE – Revised Edition – St. Francis de Sales – Translated by Msgr. John K. Ryan (D301) – $1.75
TOWARD A NEW CATHOLIC MORALITY – John Giles Milhaven (D302) – $1.45
THE POWER AND THE WISDOM – John L. McKenzie (D303) – $1.75
INFALLIBLE? AN INQUIRY – Hans Küng (D304 – $1.45
THE DECLINE AND FALL OF RADICAL CATHOLICISM – James Hitchcock (D305) – $1.25
IN THE SPIRIT, IN THE FLESH – Eugene C. Kennedy (D306) – $1.25
THE THIRD PEACOCK – Robert Farrar Capon (D307) – $1.25
THE GOD OF SPACE AND TIME – Bernard J. Cooke (D308) – $1.45
AN AQUINAS READER (Image Original) – Edited with an Intro. by Mary T. Clark (D309) – $2.45

These prices subject to change without notice

A 74-5